ROSA'S
THAI CAFE

12

An Hachette UK Company
www.hachette.co.uk

First published in Great Britain in 2015 by
Mitchell Beazley, a division of Octopus Publishing Group Ltd
Endeavour House
189 Shaftesbury Avenue
London
WC2H 8JY
www.octopusbooks.co.uk

ISBN 978 1 84533 953 1

A CIP catalogue record for this book is available from the British Library

Printed and bound in China
10 9 8 7 6 5 4 3 2 1

PUBLISHING DIRECTOR
Stephanie Jackson
DEPUTY ART DIRECTOR
Yasia Leedham-Williams
PROJECT EDITOR
Alex Stetter
DESIGN
BuroCreative
PHOTOGRAPHY
Dan Jones
PROP STYLIST
Jessica Georgiades
ASSISTANT PRODUCTION MANAGER
Lucy Carter

ROSA'S THAI CAFE

THE COOKBOOK

BORN IN THE EAST.
RAISED IN THE
EAST END.

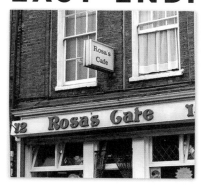

One day in 2008 I was walking up Brick Lane with my husband and we stumbled across a disused old English caff in Spitalfields called Rosa's. We fell in love with it, as it seemed like the perfect location in which to sell my food: it was a fusion of cool, authentic London and modern Bangkok. It was to be the place where Rosa's Thai Café was born.

The story of Rosa's Thai Café really began in a very small town called Khao Khor (it has grown a bit since I lived there) in Phetchaboon province, northern Thailand. This is where I was born into a loving, simple family – I have two sisters and one brother – and where my ancestors have been farmers for generations. I believe this set the foundation for my culinary ambitions. I was surrounded by fresh, locally grown produce that I used to cook and eat from a very young age. I would wake up at 5 a.m. to go to the local market and buy ingredients for that day's lunch. I remember the first thing I ever cooked was sticky rice.

When I turned 14, I set up my own noodle stall. I was able to pay for my studies with the income, so I guess that noodle stall was my first entrepreneurial venture. When I graduated from college four years later, I set my sights on Hong Kong – this was a huge step for me, as I'd never even left the Thai countryside. When I arrived in Hong Kong, I lived with a Chinese family and I got a part-time job working in a Thai restaurant. I soon realized I wanted to do more than cut vegetables in the kitchen of a Thai restaurant, especially since I knew I could create delicious food. In 1994, I set about opening my own Thai grocery shop in Hong Kong, which took off thanks to the influx of Thai expats at the time. Once I had made enough money, I sold up and created my first ever restaurant – well, actually it was a takeaway, but it sold the food I made, which was all that mattered to me. In 2004 I finally opened my first real restaurant: Tuk Tuk Thai had actual seats, which was a big deal for me. I adored my creation (which is still open today), so I was incredibly reluctant to say yes when my husband asked if we were ready to move to London.

Touching down in London in 2006 was frightening, to say the least. 'What am I to do?' was the question that went through my head for the entire 13-hour plane journey. Starting from scratch again was daunting; it took all my courage to create a new venture, as I thought I would not be able to top Tuk Tuk Thai in Hong Kong. Finally, I started my catering company Chic, for which I cooked all the food on four electric burners in my very own kitchen. I had a few notable clients, including Red Bull and the Thai Tourism Authority, among others. I have to thank all my friends for the amount of business they put my way: their much-needed support gave me enough capital to finally create, yes, you got it, Rosa's Thai Café. The rest is history.

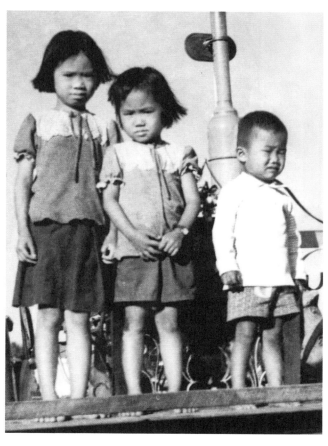

THE FLAVOURS OF THAI COOKING

All of Thai cooking is based around four flavours: salty, spicy, sour and sweet. Every dish in Thai cuisine incorporates at least two of them, and sometimes all four. The art lies in striking the perfect balance. One flavour may be dominant, but the others will be there too, like notes in a chord. A dish may be sweet, but it will still have the essence of at least one other flavour. No single flavour is ever allowed completely to overpower the others. You must always be able to taste all the flavours, singly and in unison.

Many of the dishes in this book are cooked in a wok and come together very quickly – it might take you longer to chop and prepare the ingredients than to cook the actual dish! For best results, it's important not to over-fill your wok – your ingredients will get steamed and soggy rather than stir-fried and crispy. A number of recipes in this book therefore serve only two people, but if you are cooking for more, I suggest you scale up the ingredients as necessary, get everything ready, and then cook your chosen dish in two or three batches. It won't take long, and every serving will be just as delicious.

INGREDIENTS

In Thai cooking there are many different ingredients that you may not have come across before, from galangal to holy basil. The best place to find these is in Asian supermarkets. However,

if you don't have a local Asian shop, you can try your nearest large supermarket, where you should be able to find some of the ingredients you need. Alternatively, you can buy many of these ingredients online. See the following list for the some of the more exotic ingredients you will encounter in this book. If you can't find some of the more unusual ones, don't worry as you can easily substitute many of them with more common items.

BASIL: There are two kinds of basil used in this book: Thai basil and holy basil, both cultivars of sweet (Mediterranean) basil. Thai basil has purple stems with smaller and darker green leaves than its parent plant, but is similar at first glance, so is sometimes called Thai sweet basil, even though it has a licorice-like flavour. It is used extensively in Thai salads, soups and stir-fries. Holy basil has a much sharper, more peppery taste than Thai basil, and is therefore often called 'hot basil'. Leaves of holy basil are used to add a fiery depth and clove-like flavour to stir-fries and other Thai dishes.

CHILLIES: Thai food is impossible to imagine without chillies of all sizes and colours, used fresh, dried or roasted. Commonly used types include long or spur chillies (prik chil faa), and the much smaller bird's eye chillies (prik kii nuu suan). Dried chillies are usually soaked in water before use to soften them. A lot of the dishes in this book are hot and spicy: in Thai cooking, we use chillies plus the seeds for that extra kick. However, if you aren't such a fan of spicy food, reduce the amount of chilli in the recipe and remember to deseed the pods when you're chopping them up.

CHINESE CELERY: Chinese celery has thinner stems than regular celery and its leaves are used as much as its stalks. It has a stronger flavour than the European variety and is seldom, if ever, eaten raw. Instead, it is most commonly chopped and added to soups and stir-fries.

CORIANDER ROOT: In Thai cooking every part of the coriander plant is used, including the root, which is one of the base ingredients of many Thai curry pastes. The roots can also be chopped finely and used to season broths, sauces and rice, or pounded into a paste that can be used as a marinade. If you can't find coriander root at your Asian supermarket, use the stalks instead – try using 5 stalks for every root, as their flavour is milder.

FISH SAUCE (NAM PLA): The idea of fermenting small fish with salt may not sound very appealing, but fish sauce is the condiment that makes so many Thai dishes come to life and I can't imagine cooking without it.

GALANGAL: Although this knobbly root comes from the ginger family, it is lighter in colour and tastes far more peppery. There are two types of galangal: greater galangal (usually known simply as galangal) and lesser galangal. Slightly confusingly, lesser galangal has the more pungent peppery flavour of the two. Before using fresh galangal, you will need to peel it and take off the top layer. It is then prepared either by crushing it after slicing it or by cutting it into matchstick-thin strips.

GREEN PEPPERCORNS: These are young berries from a tropical vine native to India. The peppercorns start off bright green and get darker as they ripen. They are full of heat, highly aromatic and mildly tart. In Southeast Asia, short sections of stems are added to stir-fries, dry curries, sauces and soups.

LIME LEAVES: Sometimes known as kaffir lime leaves, these leaves originate from the wild lime tree and are used to add a distinctive citrus scent to soups and curries. Used in much the same way as bay leaves, they are widely available, and you can buy them fresh or dried.

MAKRUT LIMES: Sometimes known as kaffir limes, these dark green limes have a bumpy, knobbly skin and smell absolutely wonderful.

PANDAN LEAVES: These long, glossy, dark green leaves are a key flavouring in many Southeast Asian desserts and drinks. The leaves are also used in savoury dishes, perhaps to wrap around food, such as pieces of chicken, or to infuse a sauce with their flavour in much the same way as a bouquet garni. Cooking with pandan leaves not only adds a unique flavour and subtle aroma but also adds a distinctive bright green hue.

PEA AUBERGINES: These small green aubergines are about the size of grapes and, like them, also grow in clusters. Pea aubergines are worth tracking down for their wonderfully crunchy texture.

TAMARIND: The fruit of the tamarind tree lends a distinctive sweet and tart flavour to dishes such as Pad Thai. Tamarind pulp can be processed to make a ready-to-use paste or pressed into sticky black blocks. This tamarind concentrate, available from Asian supermarkets, can easily be reconstituted with water and lasts much longer than commercially made pastes. It tastes much better, too, so that is what I suggest you use.

TARO: Taro roots need to be scrubbed and peeled before you can cook their creamy, starchy flesh. Do wear gloves when you are preparing them, as the raw flesh can cause an allergic reaction. Fresh taro is readily available, but you can also sometimes find ready-prepared frozen taro chunks at Asian supermarkets.

THAI AUBERGINES: Usually white, green or pale yellow, Thai aubergines are about the size of a golf ball. Although they are slightly bitter, they readily absorb the flavours of the sauce in which they are cooked and are therefore frequently used in Southeast Asian curries. They can also be sliced and stir-fried or grilled, and tender young Thai aubergines can even be eaten raw, unlike the more common large purple varieties.

ROASTED/TOASTED RICE: This adds a nutty flavour to many Thai dishes and also a slightly crunchy texture. It can be easily prepared at home by dry-frying a few tablespoons of uncooked basmati rice in a wok or frying pan over a low heat, stirring continuously, until golden brown, then pounding it in a mortar. However, you can also buy commercially prepared roasted rice powder from specialist suppliers.

THAI CURRY

I have included recipes for a number of different Thai curry pastes in this book, from the basic red, yellow and green pastes to Penang curry and the famous Massaman curry (see pages 202–04). However, if you don't have the time or inclination to buy all the ingredients you will need to make curry paste from scratch at home, you can use any good shop-bought curry paste of your choice.

Many traditional Thai curries, especially green curries, are cooked with coconut milk. This gives a thin, almost soupy consistency, but that doesn't mean a lack of flavour. With the right aromatics in the right quantities, a thin curry can taste just as intense as a thick one. Thick Thai curries are usually cooked with coconut cream instead of coconut milk, which gives a heavier, richer sauce, perfect on a cold evening in Britain!

1 THAI BASIL	9 PEPPERCORNS
2 PEA AUBERGINES	10 GALANGAL
3 THAI AUBERGINES	11 LESSER GALANGAL
4 CHILLIES	12 LEMON GRASS
5 HOLY BASIL	13 YARD-LONG BEANS
6 LIME	14 CHINESE CHIVES
7 LIME LEAVES	15 PANDAN LEAVES
8 CHINESE CELERY	

ROSA'S THAI CAFE DOILY

At first glance, the Rosa's doily is quintessentially British, but if you look closely, you'll see that it is packed full of images that all have their own reasons for being there. In the end, all these little stories create the larger doily itself, and represent the story of Rosa's Thai Café.

The stacks of noodle bowls around the outside represent the first noodle shop I set up, my very first venture, you could say. All the way up in the hills of Thailand, I sold my homemade broth noodles to the weary farmers. The noodle bowls are piled up on the roofs of tuk tuks, a reference not only to Bangkok's most iconic form of transport, but also to my first-ever restaurant, which I opened in Hong Kong and called Tuk Tuk Thai. The clouds of flowers that emerge from the exhaust pipes of those little three-wheeled motorized rickshaws are of course a homage to Rosa's Thai Café, but if you look closely, you will see that there are bottles enclosed in the rings of flowers. You can probably guessed what they are filled with: one of Thailand's largest exports, Sriracha sauce.

The row of monkeys holding spoons and forks are cheekily placed in the inner circle in honour of my birthday, which is in the year of the monkey according to the Chinese calendar. The cutlery is also a reference to the way we eat in Thailand – where I grew up, we only ever used chopsticks to eat noodles. At a Thai meal, you'll be given a spoon and a fork: the spoon is used in place of a knife, so it's held in the right hand (or in the left, if you're left-handed). Apart from the spoons and forks, there are salt cellars between the monkeys on our doily, and above their heads you'll see a row of very British teapots, to go with the ring of little crowns at their feet.

SMALL BITES

THAI CALAMARI
18

FISH CAKE MOUSSE
20

PRAWN WITH
GARLIC AND GREEN
PEPPERCORNS
23

CHICKEN WRAPPED
IN PANDAN LEAF
24

MINCED CHICKEN
KRA POW PUFF PASTRY
26

LARB SPRING ROLLS
28

SPICY FRIED MINCED
PORK PATTIES
30

ROTI WITH MINCED BEEF
AND BASIL LEAVES
32

THAI CALAMARI

SERVES 2

I squid, about 200g
(7oz), cleaned and slit
open lengthways

3 coriander roots,
roughly chopped

I lemon grass stalk, trimmed
and roughly chopped

I pandan leaf, roughly chopped

2 tablespoons dark soy sauce

I tablespoon oyster sauce

½ tablespoon granulated sugar

5 tablespoons cornflour

I egg, beaten

2 tablespoons water

475ml (16fl oz) vegetable
oil, for deep-frying

Sweet Chilli Sauce (see page
210) or steamed rice, to serve

FOR THE TOPPING

2 tablespoons vegetable oil

½ green pepper, cored,
deseeded and sliced

½ onion, roughly chopped

I red chilli, deseeded and
roughly chopped

2 lime leaves, roughly torn

When I lived in Hong Kong I would frequent one of the many Chinese restaurants in Lantau Island's Mui Wo, which was a healthy hike from my house. This restaurant was my finish line at the end of a busy day, and I would always order fried calamari as a 'well done' snack for myself. I've tried to replicate that dish because it makes the perfect treat.

Open the body tube of the squid out flat and score the inside of the flesh in a diamond pattern. Cut into diagonal slices. Pat the squid pieces dry with kitchen paper and set aside.

Coarsely pound together the coriander roots, lemon grass and pandan leaf using a mortar and pestle. Set aside.

Mix the soy sauce, oyster sauce and sugar in a bowl. In another bowl, mix the cornflour and beaten egg, then add this to the soy sauce mixture. Stir in the coriander root paste and mix in the water to make a batter. Add the squid pieces, mix to coat well and set aside.

To make the topping, heat the oil in a frying pan set over a medium heat, add the pepper, onion, chilli and lime leaves and cook for about 5 minutes, until the vegetables have softened.

Meanwhile, heat the oil in a wok. When it is hot, add the squid pieces one by one and deep-fry for 2–3 minutes until golden and crispy (you may need to fry the squid in batches).

Drain on kitchen paper, top with the vegetable mixture and serve hot with Sweet Chilli Sauce or rice.

FISH CAKE MOUSSE

SERVES 2–4

250g (8oz) minced fish

2 tablespoons coconut milk

1 tablespoon Red Curry Paste (see page 202)

1 tablespoon finely chopped yard-long beans (Chinese long beans)

1 egg, beaten

1 tablespoon finely sliced lesser galangal

1 tablespoon nam pla (Thai fish sauce)

3 lime leaves, finely sliced

1 teaspoon granulated sugar

2 tablespoons cornflour

Vegetable oil, for shallow-frying

TO GARNISH

2–4 sprigs of coriander

Small red chillies

TO SERVE

Sweet Chilli Sauce (see page 210)

Finely chopped cucumber

Crushed toasted peanuts

You could call this fusion dish a sister recipe to traditional Thai fish cakes, but it has a stronger taste. The coconut milk gives the patties a denser texture and slightly sweeter taste. Ready-minced fish, such as frozen spotted featherback, is available from Asian supermarkets, but you can use any white fish of your choice and mince it using a food processor. These patties are great as a starter or snack.

....

Put the fish into a large bowl and add the remaining ingredients. Stir the mixture very well until it forms a thick paste. Pinch off a bit of the paste that is about the size of a walnut and roll it into a ball with your hands. Now flatten the ball ever so slightly to form a pattie and place this on a plate. Continue until there is no paste remaining. You should have enough for 7–8 patties.

Heat enough oil in a wok to shallow-fry the patties over a medium heat. Fry the fish cakes in batches until they are golden brown – about 3–5 minutes on each side should do the trick. Drain on kitchen paper and leave to cool for a couple of minutes before serving.

Garnish with the coriander and chillies, then serve with a bowl of the dipping sauce, sprinkled with some chopped cucumber and crushed toasted peanuts.

PRAWN WITH GARLIC AND GREEN PEPPERCORNS

SERVES 2

4 large garlic cloves

20 dried white peppercorns

2 tablespoons vegetable oil

10 large prawns, shelled, deveined, heads and tails removed

1 tablespoon nam pla (Thai fish sauce)

1 teaspoon granulated sugar

15g (½oz) fresh green peppercorns (about 4 sprigs), cut into 2.5cm (1 inch) pieces

2 spring onions or 1 head of fresh young green garlic with leaves, sliced

1 long red chilli, finely chopped

Chopped fresh coriander leaves, to garnish

This dish is a good choice for a starter (I sometimes make it at Christmas) and is very simple to put together. Please don't skimp on the garlic, and I suggest you use large river prawns and let them soak up all the lovely garlic-infused oil.

Using a mortar and pestle, crush the garlic cloves and white peppercorns together.

Heat the oil in a wok over a medium heat. When the oil is hot, add the garlic and white peppercorns, prawns, fish sauce and sugar. Stir-fry until the prawns are almost cooked, then add the green peppercorns, spring onion and chilli, stir well and remove from the heat. Serve immediately, garnished with the coriander leaves.

CHICKEN WRAPPED IN PANDAN LEAF

MAKES 8 PIECES

3 coriander roots

200g (7oz) boneless, skinless chicken breast, cut into 8 chunks

I tablespoon Red Curry Paste (see page 202)

I tablespoon sesame oil

I tablespoon nam pla (Thai fish sauce)

I tablespoon granulated sugar

I tablespoon coconut milk

8 medium-sized pandan leaves

250ml (8fl oz) vegetable oil, for shallow-frying

Siricha sauce (see page 208), to serve

The first restaurant I worked in as a waitress was, of course, a Thai restaurant, and this dish was served there. Anytime it was ordered, I was the one who had to make it, and it was ordered a lot. So be warned! Once you make this dish for your family or guests, you might find yourself making it over and over again. The pandan leaf wrappers give the chicken a subtle but distinctive taste. You can actually eat the leaves along with the chicken, but it's one of those tastes people either love or hate, so unwrap the parcels if you prefer.

Crush the coriander roots using a pestle and mortar and set aside.

Place the chicken pieces in a large bowl. Add the curry paste, then pour in the sesame oil and fish sauce. Add the sugar, smashed coriander roots and coconut milk. Mix well to ensure all the chicken pieces are coated.

Now carefully wrap each piece of chicken in a pandan leaf and secure the parcel with a cocktail stick. Leave the chicken in the refrigerator for around I hour to marinate.

Heat the oil in a frying pan set over a medium heat. Add the wrapped chicken pieces and fry gently until cooked through. Drain on kitchen paper and serve immediately with the Siricha sauce.

MINCED CHICKEN KRA POW PUFF PASTIES

MAKES 4 PASTIES

3 garlic cloves

2 small red Thai chillies

2 tablespoons vegetable oil

250g (8oz) minced chicken

1 tablespoon oyster sauce

1 tablespoon light soy sauce

½ teaspoon dark soy sauce

1 teaspoon nam pla
(Thai fish sauce)

1½ teaspoons sugar

Pinch of ground white pepper

150g (5oz) yard-long beans
(Chinese long beans),
finely chopped

1 small white onion,
finely chopped

¼ red pepper, finely chopped

¼ green pepper, finely chopped

Handful of Thai basil,
finely chopped

3 lime leaves, chopped

2 tablespoons chicken
stock (optional)

1 sheet of ready-made puff
pastry (about 325g/11oz)

1 egg, beaten

The idea for this recipe hit me when I bought a Cornish pasty at London's Liverpool Street Station one day and wondered how it would turn out if I filled puff pastry with Thai minced Kra Pow instead of beef and black pepper. So I scrapped whatever I was doing that day, went home and made these pasties. They were phenomenal and, to be honest, I think I'm on to something here.

Pound the garlic and chilli together using a mortar and pestle. Set aside.

Heat a wok over a medium heat, add the vegetable oil and, when it is hot, add the minced chicken and stir-fry for 1 minute. Add the pounded garlic mixture, then stir in the oyster sauce, soy sauces, fish sauce and sugar. Sprinkle in the white pepper, then add the beans, onion, red and green peppers, basil and lime leaves and stir-fry for about 3 minutes until the chicken is cooked. If the mixture is too dry, add the stock. When the chicken is done, remove it from the heat and set aside.

Preheat the oven to 180°C/350°F/Gas mark 4.

Unroll the puff pastry sheet and cut it into quarters. Then cut each piece in half again so that you end up with 8 oblong pieces of equal size. Divide the chicken mixture between 4 of the pieces. Brush a little beaten egg around the edge, then top with the remaining pieces of pastry. Use a fork to crimp and seal the edges. Place the pasties on a baking sheet and brush the tops with beaten egg. Bake for 10–15 minutes until they are golden brown.

Remove the puffs from the oven and transfer them to a wire rack to cool slightly, until they are crispy on the outside.

LARB SPRING ROLLS

**MAKES 10 LARGE ROLLS
OR 15 SMALL ROLLS**

10–15 sheets of spring
roll rice paper

1 egg white

475ml (16fl oz) vegetable
oil, for deep-frying

Sweet Chilli Sauce (see page
210) or Fresh Spring Roll
Sauce (see page 211), to serve

FOR THE FILLING

200g (7oz) minced
pork or chicken

250g (8oz) glass noodles,
cut into short pieces
using scissors

3 tablespoons lime juice

2 tablespoons nam pla
(Thai fish sauce)

1 teaspoon dried chilli flakes

3 sprigs of coriander, chopped

3 shallots, thinly sliced

2 tablespoons roasted rice
(available from Asian
supermarkets or see page 13)

Larb, a flavoursome dish of minced meat, is originally from the Isan district of Thailand, which is famous for its sour and spicy flavours. Spring rolls are a common snack throughout Thailand, but I thought it might spice things up to add some larb to make a fiery filling. Sometimes a simple addition can make a big difference.

First make the filling by combining all the ingredients for it in a large bowl. Divide the filling into 10–15 equal portions.

Place a spring roll wrapper on a work surface with a corner pointing towards you. Brush the edges of the wrapper with the egg white. Put a portion of the filling into the centre, then fold the bottom corner over the filling. Fold in the 2 sides, then roll up to make a small log-shaped parcel. Make sure to seal the edges of the spring roll with the egg white. Repeat with the remaining filling and rice paper sheets.

Heat the oil into a deep-fat fryer or a stable wok. When the oil is hot, deep-fry the rolls over a high heat for approximately 5 minutes until they are golden. Drain on kitchen paper, then serve with Sweet Chilli Sauce or Fresh Spring Roll Sauce.

SPICY FRIED MINCED PORK PATTIES

MAKES 4-6 PATTIES

300g (10oz) minced pork

3 small red onions or ½ large onion, thinly sliced

3 garlic cloves, chopped

Small bunch of coriander, finely chopped

2 tablespoons lime juice

2 lemon grass stalks, sliced into circles

1 tablespoon chilli flakes

2 tablespoons nam pla (Thai fish sauce)

3 lime leaves, shredded

2 tablespoons roasted rice (available from Asian supermarkets or see page 13)

Vegetable oil, for shallow-frying

Side salad, to serve

A decade ago I met a lady who worked as a cook on a yacht. We struck up a conversation about food (obviously) and began jotting down each other's recipes. This dish was one of hers. The patties are delicious – they're crisp on the outside and succulent on the inside, and the herbs combine in such a way that all your taste buds tingle!

Mix all the ingredients except in the oil in a large bowl, using your hands to blend everything evenly. Divide the mixture into 4–6 portions. Roll each portion into a ball, then flatten it slightly into a pattie shape.

Heat enough oil for shallow-frying in a wok over a medium heat. When hot, shallow-fry the patties for about 2 minutes on each side, or until they are cooked through. Drain on kitchen paper, then serve with a side salad.

ROTI WITH MINCED BEEF AND BASIL LEAVES

SERVES 2

2 red chillies, finely sliced

3 garlic cloves, finely sliced

2 tablespoons vegetable oil

250g (8oz) minced beef

2 lime leaves, shredded

1 tablespoon oyster sauce

1 tablespoon light soy sauce

½ teaspoon dark soy sauce

½ tablespoon nam pla (Thai fish sauce)

1 teaspoon sugar

2 yard-long beans (Chinese long beans), cut into 2.5cm (1 inch) pieces

¼ onion, sliced

1 red chilli, diagonally sliced

3 sprigs of Thai basil

2 rotis or naan breads, to serve

This dish is essentially a meat wrap with Thai flavours, rotis being the Southeast Asian equivalent of flour tortillas. If you have trouble getting hold of them, you can simply use naan breads instead.

Pound the finely sliced chillies with the garlic using a mortar and pestle (there's no need to be too thorough).

Place a wok over a high heat. When the pan is hot, add the oil and the chilli mixture and stir-fry until it is fragrant. Now add the minced beef and stir-fry for 30 seconds. Add the lime leaves, oyster sauce, soy sauces, fish sauce and sugar. Throw in the beans, onion and diagonally sliced chilli and stir-fry for a further 30 seconds or until the beef is browned and cooked through. Stir in the basil leaves and take the wok off the heat.

Preheat a griddle pan or grill. When hot, warm the rotis or naan breads and serve with the minced beef.

SALADS

PAPAYA SALAD
36

GREEN MANGO SALAD
38

SWEDE SALAD
WITH THAI DRESSING
40

SPICY SEAFOOD SALAD
42

SOFT SHELL
CRAB SALAD
44

SPICY GRILLED
PRAWN SALAD WITH
LEMON GRASS
46

SPICY GLASS
NOODLE SALAD
48

TUNA SALAD
ON LETTUCE
50

MINCED CHICKEN SALAD
52

SMOKED DUCK
BREAST SALAD WITH
THAI DRESSING
54

YAM YAI SALAD
56

SPICY PORK
SALAD WITH
CHINESE KALE
58

SPICY GRILLED
BEEF SALAD
60

PAPAYA SALAD

SERVES 2

2 tablespoons peanuts

10 red bird's eye chillies or 2 large red chillies

5 small (or 2–3 large) garlic cloves

1½ tablespoons palm sugar

2 yard-long beans (Chinese long beans), cut into 2.5cm (1 inch) pieces

4 cherry tomatoes, sliced

2 tablespoons fresh lime juice

2 tablespoons nam pla (Thai fish sauce)

½ medium green papaya, peeled and shredded

1 carrot, shredded

2 tablespoons dried shrimp

Even if you've never been to Thailand, I'm sure you'll have heard of this famous salad. It seems to me I've been eating it since I was born. You could say I grew up with the taste of shredded papaya. This is a family recipe and making it is second nature to me. It was our equivalent of an English Sunday roast, except we ate it every day. My family even matched my age to the number of chillies they used (five chillies when I was five years old and so on). This trained me to enjoy the wonderful stinging heat of chillies.

In a small dry frying pan, toast the peanuts over a medium heat until golden brown. Remove from the pan and set aside.

Coarsely pound the chillies and garlic together using a pestle and mortar. Add the palm sugar, beans and tomatoes. Lightly pound to combine, then squeeze in the lime juice and fish sauce. Lightly pound again, then add the green papaya and carrot. Pound again and toss to combine. The taste should be sweet and salty in perfect balance, with a sharp, sour and spicy tang.

Spoon the salad into a serving bowl and sprinkle over the dried shrimp and toasted peanuts.

GREEN MANGO SALAD

SERVES 2

2 tablespoons dried shrimp

6 prawns, shelled, deveined and heads removed

I slightly unripe mango, cut into very thin strips

Handful of fresh coriander leaves, chopped, to serve

FOR THE SPICY DRESSING

2 tablespoons nam pla (Thai fish sauce)

I tablespoon palm sugar

2 small hot red Thai chillies, finely chopped

2 shallots, sliced

Whenever a storm hit my home town, the winds were so fierce that unripe mangoes would fall from the trees, which was quite a hazard. Once the storm cleared, there would be a plethora of unripe mangoes scattered about, ready for the taking. As the saying goes, 'waste not, want not', so after each storm we would gather the mangoes and make this dish. Sometimes a storm would last for days; I recall one week full of crunchy mangoes – it was the best week of my life!

Soak the dried shrimp in warm water for 2 minutes, then drain and set aside.

Place the cleaned prawns in boiling water over a medium heat until they are cooked through, then drain and set aside.

To prepare the dressing, combine the fish sauce and palm sugar in a bowl and stir until the sugar dissolves. Add the chillies and shallots and mix well.

Put the mango and cooked prawns into a bowl. Pour over the dressing, mix well, then serve immediately, topped with the fresh coriander and reserved shrimp.

SWEDE SALAD WITH THAI DRESSING

SERVES 2

1 carrot, shredded

½ swede (about 125g/4oz),
    peeled and shredded

1 green apple, shredded

¼ spring cabbage, shredded

½ cucumber, cored
    and thinly sliced

½ green pepper, sliced

½ red pepper, sliced

1 red onion, sliced

Bunch of mint, chopped

Bunch of coriander, chopped

FOR THE DRESSING

3 red chillies, very
    finely chopped

3 garlic cloves, finely chopped

3 tablespoons lime juice

2 tablespoons nam pla
    (Thai fish sauce)

1 tablespoon palm sugar

When I lived in Jersey, there was only one Chinese shop that sold oriental produce. I had to order in papaya, which this dish is usually made with. That option was very expensive and the order would take around a month to arrive, so I often made do with the local produce, and swede worked a treat in this dish. If you are feeling adventurous, chop up a packet of lightly smoked salmon and add it to the mix.

First make the dressing by mixing all the ingredients for it in a small bowl.

Put all the remaining ingredients in a salad bowl, pour over the dressing, mix well and serve.

SPICY SEAFOOD SALAD

SERVES 2

1 squid, about 200g
(7oz), cleaned and slit
open lengthways

6 prawns, shelled, deveined
and heads removed,
but with tails intact

6 mussels

4 scallops, sliced into bite-
sized pieces if large

1 lemon grass stalk, sliced

2–3 shallots, sliced

1 tablespoon sliced red chillies

1 Little Gem lettuce,
leaves separated

1 Chinese celery stick, sliced

1 spring onion, sliced

4 cherry tomatoes, cut in half

FOR THE DRESSING

2 tablespoons nam pla
(Thai fish sauce)

3 tablespoons lime juice

1 tablespoon granulated sugar

2 tablespoons evaporated milk

1 teaspoon roasted chilli
paste (available from
Asian supermarkets)

In my home town we used fish in just about every dish we ever made. In my restaurant in Hong Kong, I decided to toss together a Thai salad with a dressing that went back to my childhood. I figured the original dressing would be a little sour for Western palates, so I sweetened it a bit. The resulting dish was extremely popular as a lunch or light dinner. The salad should be well spiced, with a sour aroma and a taste that balances sweet and salty. You can use any combination of seafood you like, such as mussels and crab meat.

To prepare the dressing, combine the fish sauce, lime juice and sugar in a small dish. Stir until the sugar dissolves, then mix in the evaporated milk and roasted chilli paste. Set aside.

Open out the squid, score the inside of the flesh in a diamond pattern, then cut into diagonal slices. Pat the squid pieces dry with kitchen paper and set aside.

Blanch the squid, prawns, mussels and scallops in boiling water over a medium heat for about 1½ minutes. Once the seafood is cooked, drain it immediately and place in a mixing bowl. Add the remaining ingredients to the bowl. Pour over the dressing, then toss to combine thoroughly. Serve immediately.

SOFT SHELL CRAB SALAD

SERVES 2

½ iceberg lettuce, shredded

10 cherry tomatoes, sliced

½ cucumber, sliced

2 lemon grass stalks, sliced

Large handful of fresh
coriander leaves, chopped

Handful of mint leaves

lime wedges, to serve

FOR THE DEEP-FRIED CRAB

Vegetable oil, for deep-frying

4 soft shell crabs

1 egg, whisked

2 teaspoons cornflour

FOR THE DRESSING

3 tablespoons nam pla
(Thai fish sauce)

1 teaspoon sugar

3 tablespoons lime juice

5 hot red spur chillies, crushed

2 garlic cloves, crushed

My restaurant in Hong Kong was named Tuk Tuk Thai, after Thailand's famous auto-rickshaws, and I created this salad to be served there. As the crab is fried, I decided to add it to a salad rather than a curry to keep the crunch. With a dressing from my home town, it was perfect. I usually deep-fry the crabs but you could shallow-fry them instead if you like.

First, prepare the crabs. Heat a one-third depth of oil in a wok or deep-fat fryer. Brush the crabs with whisked egg, then coat with the cornflour. Deep-fry the crabs until golden brown, then drain on kitchen paper. When they are cool enough to handle, break the crabs into substantial pieces and set aside.

To prepare the dressing, combine all the ingredients for it in a bowl. Stir until the sugar dissolves.

Toss together the lettuce, tomatoes, cucumber and lemon grass in a salad bowl, adding the dressing, coriander and mint as you toss. Keep tossing until well mixed, then add the pieces of crab.

Pour over the dressing, mix well and serve with lime wedges.

SPICY GRILLED PRAWN SALAD WITH LEMON GRASS

SERVES 2

6 freshwater prawns,
  shelled and deveined

3 shallots, sliced

4 garlic cloves, thinly sliced

4 lemon grass stalks, trimmed
  and thinly sliced

Handful of mint
  leaves, chopped

Bunch of spring onions,
  thinly sliced

Handful of coriander
  leaves, chopped

FOR THE DRESSING

7 red bird's eye chillies

5 garlic cloves

4 tablespoons lime juice

2 tablespoons nam pla
  (Thai fish sauce)

1 tablespoon caster sugar

Lemon grass is a very healthy herb and it also packs a wonderful flavour punch, which can be overpowering if not added carefully. In a Thai salad, we use it fresh, which gives it even more of a kick.

Preheat a grill or barbecue until very hot.

Meanwhile, prepare the dressing: put the chillies, garlic, lime juice, fish sauce and sugar into a blender or mortar and blitz or pound to a smooth paste. Set aside.

Grill or barbecue the prawns until cooked. Set aside.

Transfer the dressing to a bowl and mix well with the shallots, sliced garlic, lemon grass, mint leaves, spring onions and coriander. Mix the grilled prawns into the salad and serve.

SPICY GLASS NOODLE SALAD

SERVES 2

100g (3½oz) dried glass noodles

8 prawns, shelled and deveined

200g (7oz) mixed seafood, such as squid, mussels and scallops

½ onion, chopped

1 Chinese celery stick, chopped

1 small lettuce, chopped

FOR THE DRESSING

1 long red chilli, sliced

3 garlic cloves

3 tablespoons lime juice

2 tablespoons nam pla (Thai fish sauce)

1 teaspoon chopped red spur chilli

2 teaspoons brown sugar

Being very popular, this dish simply had to be included here. Of course, like many staple Thai dishes, everyone has their own take on it and this is my recipe. It is a little bit spicy, but not too much compared to some of the others out there.

Soak the glass noodles in cold water for 20 minutes. Drain and set aside.

Bring a pan of water to the boil, then add the prawns and mixed seafood and boil for roughly 3–5 minutes until it is cooked. Drain and set aside.

Make the dressing. Using a mortar and pestle or a food processor, pound or blitz the sliced long chilli and garlic into a rough paste. Mix in the lime juice, fish sauce, chopped spur chilli and brown sugar. Continue pounding or blitzing the mixture until the sugar disintegrates.

Combine the noodles, seafood and chopped vegetables with the dressing in a deep bowl and mix well. Serve immediately.

TUNA SALAD ON LETTUCE

SERVES 2

2 shallots, finely chopped

2.5cm (1 inch) piece of fresh root ginger, peeled and sliced

3 garlic cloves, finely sliced

2 lemon grass stalks, finely sliced

Large handful of mixed peppery salad leaves, such as rocket

Bunch of fresh coriander leaves, chopped

A few mint leaves, torn

2 fresh tuna steaks, about 150g (5oz) each

Small handful of dried coconut shavings, to serve

FOR THE DRESSING

2 tablespoons nam pla (Thai fish sauce)

1 red chilli, finely sliced

3 tablespoons lime juice

My family were farmers, so vegetables were plentiful in our home, and salad would make an appearance on our dining mat every night. This made me a salad lover. With this recipe I wanted to create a Thai take on the French Niçoise. My version is wonderfully light and healthy, full of flavoursome ingredients. It hasn't gained any international traction yet, but I'll let you know when it does.

Put the shallots, ginger, garlic and lemon grass into a bowl, add the salad leaves and herbs and toss to combine.

Put the ingredients for the dressing into another bowl and mix well to blend.

Preheat a griddle pan. When hot, cook the tuna steaks in it for about 45–60 seconds on each side. You want the tuna to still be a little pink in the middle. Remove from the pan and slice diagonally.

Serve the tuna on a bed of salad leaves, drizzle over the dressing and sprinkle with coconut shavings.

MINCED CHICKEN SALAD

SERVES 2

3 garlic cloves, finely chopped

3 shallots, finely chopped

3cm (1¼ inch) piece of galangal, thinly sliced

1 lemon grass stalk, thinly sliced

2–3 tablespoons vegetable oil

250g (8oz) minced chicken

1 teaspoon dried chilli powder

Pinch of salt

2 tablespoons lime juice

1 tablespoon nam pla (Thai fish sauce)

1 tablespoon roasted rice (available from Asian supermarkets or see page 13)

1 lime leaf, shredded

Handful of coriander leaves, roughly chopped

Handful of mint leaves, roughly chopped

1 spring onion, sliced

TO SERVE

Chilled wedges of iceberg lettuce

Fresh green vegetables of your choice, such as Thai aubergine and yard-long beans (Chinese long beans)

1 red chilli, sliced

My uncle was an excellent cook – he did most of the cooking in his family and he wouldn't accept anything less than perfection. His favourite recipe was Laab Gai, and his trick was to deep-fry all the ingredients (except the chicken) until crispy and golden brown. We all looked forward to this dish of spicy minced chicken, packed full of herbs and spices. The chilli powder does give the dish an incredible punch, and I think it's definitely best when it is extra spicy, but you can reduce the quantity to suit your palate.

Mix together the chopped garlic, shallots, galangal and lemon grass in a bowl.

Place the oil in a wok set over a high heat until it is extremely hot. Add the garlic mixture and stir-fry for about 2–3 minutes until golden brown.

Add the minced chicken and continue to stir-fry for about 2 minutes until the chicken is cooked through. Take the wok off the heat and add the chilli powder, salt, lime juice, fish sauce, roasted rice and the lime leaf. Stir in the coriander, mint and spring onion. Mix well and taste – it should have a delicious balance of spicy, sour and salty.

Serve with lettuce and other fresh green vegetables, sprinkled with chilli slices. The traditional way to eat Laab Gai is to wrap the hot meat in really cold lettuce leaves. Trust me, it tastes superb this way. The different flavours and temperatures just explode in your mouth!

SMOKED DUCK BREAST SALAD WITH THAI DRESSING

SERVES 2

200g (7oz) smoked duck breast

150g (5oz) mixed salad leaves

1 sprig of coriander,
    leaves chopped

1 spring onion, chopped

3 cherry tomatoes, halved

FOR THE DRESSING

1 tablespoon lime juice

1 tablespoon nam pla
    (Thai fish sauce)

1½ teaspoons brown sugar

1 teaspoon crushed
    dried red chilli

I came across some smoked duck at a local market in Hong Kong, and the beautifully pink meat made me want to make a crunchy mixed-leaf salad to go with it. The saltiness of the duck didn't work with any of the sweet dressings I tried, so I kept playing around and finally concocted this punchy sour sauce, similar to those usually used for Thai seafood. It worked!

To make the dressing, mix all the ingredients together in a large bowl and stir until the sugar has dissolved. Set aside.

Preheat a grill or griddle pan until very hot, then cook the duck breast for 3–5 minutes on each side until cooked. Cut the duck breast into slices and set aside.

Toss together the salad leaves, coriander, spring onion and cherry tomatoes, then sit the duck breast slices on top. Pour the dressing over the salad and serve immediately.

YAM YAI SALAD

SERVES 2

150g (5oz) Chinese
   cabbage, chopped

50g (2oz) Chinese
   celery, chopped

100g (3½oz) cucumber,
   cut into batons

½ white onion, chopped

2 spring onions, shredded

50g (2oz) boiled pork
   belly, sliced

20g (¾oz) dried squid, shredded

1 hardboiled egg, shelled
   and cut into quarters

5 cherry tomatoes

FOR THE SAUCE

2 red bird's eye chillies,
   chopped

2 fresh garlic cloves, crushed

2 pickled garlic cloves, chopped

1 tablespoon lime juice

1 tablespoon condensed milk

1 tablespoon nam pla
   (Thai fish sauce)

1 hardboiled egg yolk

1 teaspoon palm sugar

The name of this dish translates literally as 'big salad', and it's a Thai classic. I have been preparing it for many years, always trying to improve it and bring the different flavours into a perfect balance. My secret ingredient is shredded dried squid – a delicacy worth tracking down at specialist Asian grocers or buying online.

Start by making the sauce. Place the chillies and both types of garlic into a food processor and pulse to form a paste. Transfer the mixture to a bowl, add all the remaining ingredients for the sauce and mix well.

Now place all the salad ingredients in a large bowl and toss, adding the sauce as you do so.

SPICY PORK SALAD WITH CHINESE KALE

SERVES 2

200g (7oz) pork sirloin, sliced

3 Chinese kale (kai-lan) stems or Chinese celery sticks, chopped

Large handful of fresh coriander, roughly chopped

Large handful of mint, roughly chopped

FOR THE DRESSING

3 small red bird's eye chillies, finely chopped

4 garlic cloves, finely chopped

I tablespoon palm sugar

2 tablespoons lime juice

I teaspoon nam pla (Thai fish sauce)

Whenever there was a party in our village, there would be plenty of homemade food and a lot of homemade moonshine. I could always tell if we'd get drunk because this dish would be there, alongside countless bottles of the strong stuff. To be honest, I'm surprised I even remember the recipe, but I have to admit it is a great dish for when you're drinking – the sour tang and saltiness really wake you up!

Bring a wok or saucepan of water to the boil, then add the pork and reduce the heat. Leave the pork to simmer for 3–5 minutes, until just cooked through – do not overcook.

Meanwhile, put all the dressing ingredients in a small bowl and stir well until the sugar has dissolved.

Drain the pork. Put the Chinese kale into a serving bowl, followed by the pork, chopped coriander and mint. Toss the salad while gradually pouring over the dressing. Serve immediately.

SPICY GRILLED BEEF SALAD

SERVES 4

300g (10oz) beef tenderloin

1 onion, sliced

½ cucumber, sliced diagonally and halved

12 cherry tomatoes, halved

mixed salad leaves, shredded

FOR THE DRESSING

10 small garlic cloves

5 hot red spur chillies

3 tablespoons nam pla (Thai fish sauce)

3 tablespoons lime juice

2 tablespoons chilli sauce

1 tablespoon granulated sugar

TO SERVE

Sliced red chilli

Fresh coriander leaves

When I opened my takeaway in Hong Kong, most of my customers were British expats, who loved this beef salad. I have been preparing it for many years, always trying to improve it and bring the different flavours into perfect balance – not too sweet, salty or spicy... I keep on trying, and this is where I've got to so far. I guess this version may be as near to perfect as I can manage!

To prepare the dressing, coarsely pound the garlic and chillies together using a mortar and pestle or a food processor. Scoop the mixture into a dish and add the fish sauce, lime juice, chilli sauce and sugar. Stir until the sugar dissolves. Set aside.

Preheat a non-stick griddle pan. Wipe the beef dry and cut it into 2.5cm (1 inch) thick steaks. Cook over a medium-high heat for about 2 minutes on each side, or until the meat is done to your liking. Slice thinly.

In a mixing bowl, combine the beef, onion, cucumber and tomatoes. Pour over the dressing and add the salad leaves. Toss to combine.

Transfer to serving bowls. Garnish with sliced chilli and coriander leaves and serve immediately.

SOUPS

PRAWN SPICY
SOUR SOUP
64

THAI CHICKEN
NOODLE SOUP
66

COCONUT SOUP
WITH CHICKEN
68

KHAO KHOR
CHICKEN TOM
YUM SOUP
70

OXTAIL SOUP
72

PRAWN SPICY SOUR SOUP

SERVES 2

500ml (17fl oz) stock or water

2 slices of galangal

1 lemon grass stalk, sliced into 2.5cm (1 inch) pieces

2 red chillies, sliced

10cm (4 inch) piece of coriander root, chopped

6 prawns, deveined, shelled and heads removed, but with tails intact

20g (¾oz) oyster mushrooms, thinly sliced (optional)

1 generous teaspoon roasted chilli paste (available from Asian supermarkets)

1 tablespoon coconut milk

2 tablespoons nam pla (Thai fish sauce)

3 tablespoons lime juice

8 button mushrooms

3 cherry tomatoes, halved

Handful of coriander leaves, chopped, to garnish

Steamed rice, to serve

In my home town, prawns are rare and very expensive, so we used chicken instead in our Tom Yam. But this most famous Thai soup is traditionally made with prawns, and that's how it's served in just about every Thai restaurant in the world. When we had a get-together of locals and friends for dinner there would always be soup involved, and this would be the soup of choice. Most non-Thais think Tom Yam is a starter, but with us it has always been a main dish. Rice on the side is a must. The soup should be a fragrant, sour-spicy concoction.

Bring the stock or water to the boil in a saucepan set over a high heat. Add the galangal, lemon grass, chillies and coriander root and cook for a minute or so.

Add the prawns and oyster mushrooms, if using, then stir in the chilli paste, coconut milk, fish sauce and lime juice. Cook on a high heat until the prawns are done.

Stir in the button mushrooms and tomatoes. Garnish with chopped coriander and serve immediately with steamed rice.

THAI CHICKEN NOODLE SOUP

A staple in Thailand, this soup can be found on almost every street corner in every province. It's impossible to come across the ultimate noodle soup recipe – there are so many good ones! Each street stall serving this dish will be very proud of its own recipe, which will have been passed down the generations of the family and tweaked countless times on the way. This is my family's version.

SERVES 2

200g (7oz) rice vermicelli

3 tablespoons vegetable oil

3 garlic cloves, crushed

150g (5oz) bean sprouts

600ml (1 pint) chicken stock

1 tablespoon light soy sauce

1 tablespoon palm sugar

½ head of pickled garlic

4 coriander roots

1 pandan leaf

½ teaspoon salt

200g (7oz) boneless, skinless chicken breast

TO SERVE

1 Chinese celery stick, chopped

2 sprigs of coriander, finely chopped

2 spring onions, finely chopped

1 teaspoon dried turnip (available from Asian supermarkets)

Pinch of white pepper

Soak the rice noodles in warm water for 10 minutes, then drain.

Meanwhile, heat the oil in small saucepan over a high heat, add the garlic and cook, stirring continuously, until it is golden brown. Remove the garlic from the pan and set aside.

Bring a pan of water to a rolling boil, then add the noodles and cook for 30 seconds. Drain and place in a bowl with the bean sprouts. Set aside.

Pour the chicken stock into a deep saucepan, add the soy sauce, palm sugar, pickled garlic, coriander roots, pandan leaf and salt and bring to a low boil. Add the chicken and poach for 20 minutes, then remove from the pan, slice and set aside. If the chicken is not yet cooked through, return the slices to the pan for a minute until they are done, then remove and set aside. Simmer the soup for 2 minutes more.

Divide the noodles and bean sprouts between 2 serving bowls, then pour over the soup. The hot stock will cook the bean sprouts ever so slightly. Top with the sliced chicken and sprinkle over the Chinese celery, coriander, spring onions and dried turnip. Season with the white pepper and serve immediately.

COCONUT SOUP WITH CHICKEN

SERVES 2

500ml (17fl oz) coconut milk

4 lemon grass stalks, sliced diagonally

4 slices of galangal

3 red chillies, sliced

4 coriander roots

8 white beech (shimeji) or small button mushrooms, quartered

5 cherry tomatoes, halved

250g (8oz) boneless, skinless chicken breast, sliced into thin, bite-sized pieces

2 tablespoons nam pla (Thai fish sauce)

2 tablespoons lime juice

Coriander leaves, to garnish

Super-quick to make, this coconut soup is fantastic on a cold winter's night, not that we ever have them in Thailand. This satisfying soup always made us feel warm inside. My auntie, who had a lot of coconut trees, taught me how to cook this dish. When her coconuts ripened, there were so many, we'd have enough for a month. I must admit, I've always had a love-hate relationship with this recipe, not because of the taste (which is wonderful), but because we had to go to my friend's farm to kill a chicken to make it. And we ate it so much, this was almost a daily event. The galangal adds a unique flavour to the soup, which should be salty and sour, with a little spice.

Heat the coconut milk in a saucepan until it starts to boil. Add the lemon grass, galangal, chillies, coriander roots, mushrooms and tomatoes and stir for a minute or so.

Add the chicken and stir continuously over a high heat for 2–3 minutes until the chicken is almost done, then season with the fish sauce and lime juice. Stir over a high heat for another minute or so until the chicken is cooked all the way through. Garnish with coriander leaves and serve immediately.

KHAO KHOR CHICKEN TOM YUM SOUP

SERVES 2

1 litre (1¾ pints) water

4 medium slices of galangal (about 1cm/½ inch of root)

3 lime leaves, torn

2 lemon grass stalks, sliced

3 small shallots, chopped

3 garlic cloves, crushed

1 coriander root

150g (5oz) boneless, skinless chicken breast, sliced

3 tablespoons nam pla (Thai fish sauce)

2 tablespoons lime juice

1 teaspoon salt

½ tablespoon dried chilli flakes

3 dried chillies, halved

½ tablespoon vegetable oil

50g (2oz) oyster mushrooms

1 spring onion, sliced

1 Chinese celery stick, chopped

Handful of Thai basil

Handful of fresh coriander leaves

4 cherry tomatoes, halved

The town where I am from is called Khao Khor. It's hard to translate, but this name is a reference to what I can perhaps best describe as a 'mountain chestnut', a type of nut that grows in this region. Wild chickens would eat the nuts when they fell to the ground, so when we caught these birds for our soup, their meat had a subtle nutty flavour.

Put the measurement water into a deep saucepan set over a high heat. When it starts to boil, add the galangal, lime leaves, lemon grass, shallots, garlic and coriander root and boil for 2 minutes. Now add the chicken and cook for a further 2 minutes. Mix in the fish sauce, lime juice, salt and chilli flakes and cook for a further 3 minutes.

Meanwhile, fry the dried chillies in a little vegetable oil over a medium heat.

Ensure the chicken is cooked through, then add the mushrooms to the pan and reduce the heat to medium. The soup should taste spicy, sour and salty. Cook for 30 seconds, then stir in the fried chilli and the remaining fresh ingredients. Transfer the soup to 2 deep bowls and serve immediately.

SOUP HANG WUA

OXTAIL SOUP

SERVES 4

1 litre (1¾ pints) water

300g (10oz) oxtail or
    stewing steak

3 coriander roots

20 black peppercorns

1 teaspoon brown sugar

1 onion, chopped

2 beef tomatoes, quartered

1 large potato, chopped

1½ teaspoons salt

FOR THE SEAFOOD SAUCE

2 tablespoons nam pla
    (Thai fish sauce)

2 tablespoons lime juice

2 garlic cloves, crushed

2 dried red chillies,
    finely chopped

1 teaspoon palm sugar

1 sprig coriander, finely chopped

This recipe comes from a market stall in Bangkok. As soon as I took my first sip of the broth, I asked for the recipe, but the stallholder was reluctant to give it to me. I guess it was a family secret. But it was so good, I did my best to coerce him into sharing it! However, I'm not sure he did share the secret because, to this day, I can't make it like he did. But I've tried my best to tweak the recipe to replicate that flavour and this is what I've come up with – it's not exactly the same, but it's still wonderful.

Put the measurement water in a large saucepan over a medium heat and add the oxtail, followed by the remaining ingredients. Bring to the boil, then reduce the heat and simmer for 40 minutes.

Meanwhile, mix together all the ingredients for the sauce in a small bowl.

Serve the soup with the seafood sauce on the side, to spoon into your bowl as you eat.

CURRIES

SALMON RED CURRY
76

ROSA'S GREEN CURRY
WITH CHICKEN
78

RED CHICKEN CURRY
80

THAI-STYLE
INDIAN CHICKEN WITH
YELLOW CURRY
82

CHICKEN WITH
RED CURRY
84

ROAST DUCK CURRY
86

PORK STEWED
IN THAI GRAVY
86

BEEF MASSAMAN CURRY
90

BEEF RED CURRY
92

SALMON RED CURRY

SERVES 2

2½ tablespoons vegetable oil

2 tablespoons Red Curry Paste (see page 202)

250ml (8fl oz) coconut milk

2 tablespoons nam pla (Thai fish sauce)

I tablespoon palm sugar

2 salmon steaks, about 150g (5oz) each

Steamed rice, to serve

TO GARNISH

I lime leaf, shredded

I red spur chilli, sliced

5cm (2 inch) piece of lesser galangal, thinly sliced lengthways

Thai basil leaves, shredded

In my home town in northern Thailand, salmon is unheard of. We used to fish for catfish in small lakes surrounded by jungle. Things were different in Hong Kong, where salmon was a popular fish with the British expats. The first time I tasted it, I was hooked. I couldn't help thinking that the oily soft flesh and subtle flavour would be perfect in a curry. When cooking this curry, try to keep sweet and salty in perfect balance.

To make the sauce, heat 2 tablespoons of the oil in a wok set over a medium heat and sauté the curry paste until it is fragrant. Add 200ml (7fl oz) of the coconut milk, the fish sauce and the palm sugar and bring to the boil. Reduce the heat to medium and cook, stirring continuously, for about 3 minutes until the oil from the curry paste starts rising to the top and the mixture is smooth and thick. Add almost all the remaining coconut milk (you want to save a tablespoon for garnish). Bring to the boil again. The sauce should have a perfect balance of spicy, salty and sweet. Reduce the heat to low.

Clean the salmon, pat dry with kitchen paper and pan-fry in the remaining vegetable oil until cooked to your liking.

Place the salmon steaks on plates and pour over the curry sauce. Top with the lime leaf, chilli, galangal and basil and pour over the reserved coconut milk. Serve with steamed rice.

ROSA'S GREEN CURRY WITH CHICKEN

SERVES 4

1 tablespoon vegetable oil

3 tablespoons Green Curry Paste (see page 203)

400ml (14fl oz) coconut milk

1 tablespoon palm sugar

2 tablespoons nam pla (Thai fish sauce)

Sea salt

3 lime leaves, torn

500g (1lb) boneless, skinless chicken breast, cut into bite-sized pieces

100g (3½ oz) pea aubergines (available online or from Thai supermarkets)

100g (3½ oz) Thai aubergines, cut into quarters

150g (5oz) cooked bamboo shoots, cut into bite-size pieces

handful of Thai basil leaves

Steamed rice, to serve

TO GARNISH

2 red spur chillies, diagonally sliced

Sprigs of Thai basil

When I was first in Hong Kong, I used to cook for my employer. I made Thai dishes, but with a Chinese twist that I hadn't tried before. The reason was simple: I couldn't get all the ingredients I would use at home in Thailand, so I made the best of what I could find. Consequently, this green curry was not what I was used to, but it turned out to be the best I had ever made!

....

Heat the oil in a saucepan over a high heat and add the curry paste. Stir-fry for 10 seconds until it is fragrant. Reduce the heat to medium and add half the coconut milk. Cook for about 2 minutes until the green oil splits and rises to the surface. Now add the remaining coconut milk. Add the palm sugar and the fish sauce, then season with a pinch of salt. Stir in the lime leaves and add the chicken to the pan. Add the pea aubergines, Thai aubergines and the bamboo shoots. Cook over a medium heat for 5–7 minutes until the chicken is cooked through. Stir in the basil leaves.

Ladle into serving bowls, garnish each one with some sliced chilli and a sprig of basil and serve with steamed rice.

RED CHICKEN CURRY

SERVES 4

1 tablespoon vegetable oil

3 tablespoons Red Curry Paste (see page 202)

400ml (14fl oz) coconut milk

500g (1lb) boneless, skinless chicken breast, cut into bite-sized pieces

2 tablespoons nam pla (Thai fish sauce)

1 teaspoon palm sugar

Handful of Thai basil leaves, plus extra to garnish

Steamed rice, to serve

TO GARNISH

5 lime leaves, finely sliced

2 red spur chillies, diagonally sliced

3cm (1¼ inch) piece of lesser galangal, peeled and thinly sliced

This is a very popular curry in Thailand, and in Thai restaurants around the world too. When I was seven years old, I used to wake up at 5 a.m. every day and walk to the local market to buy this dish. I had always wanted to learn to cook it and one day I asked the lady who sold it to teach me. Reluctantly, she shared the secret. She also gave me a useful tip: keep the curry thick or you lose some of the flavour. To this day I haven't changed the way I cook red chicken curry – and I never will.

Heat the oil in a saucepan over a high heat. Add the curry paste and stir-fry for a few seconds. Pour in the coconut milk and bring to the boil, then reduce the heat to medium and cook, stirring occasionally, until the red oil rises to the surface. Add the chicken and cook for about 10 minutes until it is done.

Season with the fish sauce and palm sugar to create a slightly salty but well-balanced taste. Bring the mixture to the boil, then turn off the heat and add the basil leaves.

Ladle into serving bowls and garnish with the lime leaves, spur chillies, galangal and some more basil leaves. Serve with steamed rice.

THAI-STYLE INDIAN CHICKEN WITH YELLOW CURRY

SERVES 2

1 onion, roughly chopped

1 carrot, thickly sliced

4 garlic cloves

2.5cm (1 inch) piece of fresh root ginger, peeled and roughly chopped

250ml (8fl oz) water

3 tablespoons vegetable oil

250g (8oz) boneless, skinless chicken breast, cut into bite-sized pieces

1 tablespoon garam masala

1 teaspoon chilli powder

1 teaspoon palm sugar

1 tablespoon salt

400g (14oz) can chopped tomatoes

10 small green bird's eye chillies

Handful of chopped fresh coriander leaves

1 tomato, chopped

I tried this dish for the first time in Hong Kong, at the infamous Chungking Mansions (if you haven't heard of this mall, please read up about it – it's a fascinating city within a city) and loved its Southeast Asian flavour. So, as is my wont, I replicated it and converted it to Thai style by (drum roll...) adding chilli.

Put the onion, carrot, garlic, ginger and water in a food processor and blend to a paste.

Heat the oil in a wok over a medium heat, then add the blended ingredients and cook for 1–2 minutes. When the mixture has come to the boil, add the chicken and stir well. Add the garam masala, chilli powder, palm sugar and salt, then stir in the canned tomatoes. Mix in the green chillies and chopped coriander. Bring back to the boil, then reduce the heat. Add the chopped fresh tomato and simmer for about 40 minutes.

Spoon into serving bowls and serve immediately.

CHICKEN WITH RED CURRY

SERVES 4

3 tablespoons vegetable oil

3 tablespoons Red Curry
  Paste (see page 202)

400g (13oz) free-range boneless,
  skinless chicken breast, sliced

300ml (½ pint) chicken stock

3 lime leaves, shredded

1 teaspoon palm sugar

1 teaspoon granulated sugar

2 tablespoons nam pla
  (Thai fish sauce)

5cm (2 inches) lesser galangal,
  thinly sliced lengthways

2 bamboo shoots, washed
  and sliced (or the vegetable
  of your choice, such as
  mangetout, aubergine
  or cauliflower)

6 holy basil leaves

½ red spur chilli,
  sliced, to garnish

Steamed rice, to serve

I learned this recipe from my friends' parents when I studied in the capital city of my province. They would make the curry paste from scratch. Red curry is ubiquitous in Thailand, but this northern take on the dish will leave you a little more hot under the collar than usual! Notice that no coconut milk is used in this red curry – 'country-style' dishes from the north of Thailand are less creamy than those from the south.

....

Heat the oil in a saucepan over a medium heat. When it is hot, add the red curry paste and stir-fry for a few seconds until it is fragrant. Now add the chicken, stir-fry for about 1 minute, then add the chicken stock. Stir in the remaining ingredients and simmer over a medium heat for about 5 minutes or until the chicken is cooked through.

Garnish with the chilli and serve with steamed rice.

ROAST DUCK CURRY

SERVES 4

2 tablespoons vegetable oil

2 tablespoons Red Curry Paste (see page 202)

400ml (14fl oz) coconut milk

1 tablespoon palm sugar

1½ tablespoons nam pla (Thai fish sauce)

2 tablespoons chicken stock (optional)

½ roasted duck, deboned and cut into 1cm (½ inch) slices

4 lime leaves, torn

10 cherry tomatoes

75g (2½oz) grapes

75g (2½oz) sliced pineapple, cut into chunks

Sea salt

TO SERVE

Sprigs of Thai basil

Red spur chilli, thinly sliced

Steamed rice

I once lived on the border of Hong Kong and China, where there was a very famous local restaurant that served a delicious type of roast duck called Tai Po. I thought to myself that a red curry with this type of duck would be fantastic, and it was! If you're feeling adventurous, use venison instead of duck. This curry combines salty and sweet flavours.

Heat the oil in a small saucepan set over a medium heat and sauté the curry paste until it is fragrant. Add half the coconut milk and stir to combine. Cook for about 2 minutes until the red oil splits and rises to the surface. Now add the palm sugar and fish sauce. If the sauce seems too thick, add the stock. Stir in the roasted duck and cook for 1 minute. Pour the remaining coconut milk into the pan and bring to the boil. Add the lime leaves. Simmer for a few minutes, then add the tomatoes, grapes and pineapple. Cook for a further minute and season to taste. The curry should have a perfect balance of salty and sweet, with a slight tang.

Ladle the curry into serving bowls. Garnish each one with a basil sprig and some sliced chilli and serve immediately with steamed rice.

PORK STEWED IN THAI GRAVY

SERVES 2

1.5 litres (2½ pints) water

300g (10oz) pork sirloin

5cm (2 inch) piece of Thai celery root or coriander root

4 tablespoons brown sugar

2 tablespoons vegetable oil

2 garlic cloves, smashed

½ teaspoon ground white pepper

1 cinnamon stick

2 star anise

100g (3½oz) silken tofu, cut into cubes

1 generous tablespoon oyster sauce

4 tablespoons light soy sauce

1 tablespoon dark sweet soy sauce

1 teaspoon dark soy sauce

1 teaspoon salt

3 eggs, hard-boiled and peeled

Steamed jasmine rice, to serve

In Thailand, storing perishable goods such as raw meat was hard work if you didn't have a refrigerator. We would often cook the meat in this flavoursome homemade Thai gravy or broth. If we didn't finish it, we would reheat it the next day, although I wouldn't recommended this now. With every day that went by, the pork became even more tender, and the broth even more flavoursome, as they both continued to absorb one another's flavours.

Put the measurement water into a large saucepan and bring to the boil. Add the pork and Thai celery root and leave to simmer for about 10 minutes.

Meanwhile, set a wok over a medium-low heat. When it is hot, add the sugar and stir for about 1 minute until it becomes brown. Add the sugar to the pork mixture.

Pour 1 tablespoon of the oil into the wok, then add the garlic, white pepper, cinnamon and star anise. Stir-fry for 30 seconds, then add to the pork.

Pour the remaining oil into the wok, add the tofu and stir-fry over a medium heat until golden-brown. Stir in the oyster sauce, soy sauces and salt and leave to simmer for about 20 minutes until the pork is tender.

Remove the pork from the pan and slice thinly. Place it in a serving bowl, add the eggs and pour over some of the broth.

Serve immediately with jasmine rice.

BEEF MASSAMAN CURRY

SERVES 2

½ teaspoon cumin

5 cardamom pods

5 cloves

I small cinnamon stick or ½ teaspoon ground cinnamon

2 tablespoons tamarind pulp

2 tablespoons vegetable oil

2 generous tablespoons Massaman Curry Paste (see page 203)

3 bay leaves

I medium onion, roughly chopped or 5 very small onions, peeled and used whole

400ml (14fl oz) coconut milk, plus extra to serve

2 tablespoons palm sugar

I teaspoon caster sugar

2 tablespoons nam pla (Thai fish sauce)

I potato, peeled and cut into bite-sized pieces

200g (7oz) beef sirloin, cut into bite-sized pieces

2 tablespoons beef or vegetable stock (optional)

2 tablespoons roasted cashew nuts

5 pieces of chopped pineapple

Sea salt

Steamed rice, to serve

I first tried this curry more than 20 years ago, at the home of one of my best friends in Hong Kong. We were planning a dinner party and wondering what to cook when my friend suggested Massaman Curry. Because I was from the north of Thailand and more used to food from Laos, I didn't know how to make this particular southern Thai dish. All I knew was that you had to use palm sugar, chopped pineapple and tamarind pulp. She knew the other ingredients, so we cooked it together and it turned out very well. Later, whenever I had a party in Hong Kong, I always served Massaman Curry: it's easy to eat, not too spicy and everyone loves it!

Roast the cumin, cardamom, cloves and cinnamon in a dry frying pan set over a medium heat, stirring continuously for a few minutes, until their aroma fills the air. Crush the spices using a pestle and mortar and set aside.

Soak the tamarind pulp in 4 tablespoons of warm water for a few minutes, then stir until it becomes a thick liquid. Set aside.

Heat the oil in a saucepan over a medium-high heat. Stir in the curry paste, crushed roasted spices, bay leaves and onion and cook until it is fragrant and the oil separates and rises to the surface. Reduce the heat to medium and simmer for 2 minutes. Add half the coconut milk and stir for I minute. Add the palm sugar, caster sugar, fish sauce and a pinch of salt. Cook for a minute, then stir in the tamarind. Add the potato and the beef. Simmer for 10–15 minutes until the beef is tender.

Add the rest of the coconut milk. If the sauce still seems too dry, add a little stock. Cook for another minute until everything is mixed well, then add the nuts and pineapple. Season to taste. It should have a perfect balance of salty, sweet and sour. Ladle into a serving bowl and drizzle over a little coconut milk.

BEEF RED CURRY

SERVES 2

2 tablespoons vegetable oil

3 tablespoons Red Curry Paste (see page 202)

½ teaspoon ground cumin

½ teaspoon ground coriander

250g (8oz) rump steak, thinly sliced

100ml (3½fl oz) coconut milk

1 teaspoon palm sugar

2 tablespoons nam pla (Thai fish sauce)

50g (2oz) pea aubergines (available from Asian supermarkets)

Steamed rice, to serve

My family and I ate this dish only at the temple. My grandparents are from Laos, so the majority of our food was Lao, not Thai. But every time the day of the Buddha arrived, people would come to the temple bringing Thai home cooking for a feast during the full moon. Beef red curry, which I found sublime, always appeared. I asked a stranger for their recipe and, many years on, I'm still cooking this dish.

Heat the oil in a wok placed over a high heat. Once the oil is hot, add the curry paste – it should sizzle as soon as it hits the wok. Stir-fry for 15 seconds, then stir in the ground cumin and coriander.

Add the sliced beef to the pan and stir-fry briefly. Stir in the coconut milk, then the palm sugar and fish sauce and stir-fry until the sugar dissolves completely. Taste the mixture – it should be sweet with a hint of saltiness, and leave you a little hot under the collar. Reduce the heat to medium and cook until the beef is tender. Add a little water if the curry is too dry. Finally, add the pea aubergines and simmer for a further 2 minutes.

Serve with steamed rice.

STIR-FRIES

STIR-FRIED MORNING GLORY

SERVES 2

2 garlic cloves

I red spur chilli

2 tablespoons vegetable oil

200g (7oz) morning glory
(available from Asian
supermarkets), cut into
5cm (2 inch) pieces

I tablespoon salted soy
bean paste (available from
Asian supermarkets)

I teaspoon nam pla
(Thai fish sauce)

I tablespoon oyster sauce

I teaspoon granulated sugar

This dish is wonderfully sweet and crunchy. Morning glory,
also known as water spinach, is a vegetable from Southeast
Asia, and not to be confused with the British plant known
by the same name, which can be poisonous. If you can't find
morning glory, you can use spinach instead. Serve this as a side
dish or with steamed rice as a vegetable-based main course.

Pound the garlic and chilli together using a mortar and pestle.

Heat the oil in a wok, then stir in the garlic mixture and the
remaining ingredients and stir-fry for roughly 90 seconds
– you want the stalks to retain their crunch and bite. Serve
immediately.

THAI SWEET-AND-SOUR TOFU

SERVES 2

2 tablespoons vegetable oil

2 garlic cloves, chopped

¼ red pepper, chopped

¼ green pepper, chopped

50g (2oz) cucumber, thickly sliced

4 cherry tomatoes

¼ onion, chopped

50g (2oz) fresh pineapple, cut into cubes

2 tablespoons tomato ketchup

I tablespoon rice vinegar

½ teaspoon Chinese rice wine

I tablespoon soy sauce

½ tablespoon granulated sugar

250g (8oz) soft tofu, cut into pieces

I spring onion, chopped

The sweet-and-sour flavour is very much associated with China, but many Southeast Asian countries have their own variants. My mum taught me this one, which uses no artificial colours, so you can achieve that vibrant red associated with sweet-and-sour dishes without skimping on quality.

Heat the oil in a wok over a high heat, add the garlic and stir-fry for about 10 seconds until golden brown. Add the red and green peppers, cucumber, tomatoes, onion and pineapple, then stir in the tomato ketchup. Add the rice vinegar, Chinese wine, soy sauce and sugar and stir to mix well. Add the tofu and stir-fry for 30 seconds, then serve topped with the spring onion.

SEAFOOD PAD CHA

SERVES 2-3

1 tablespoon sliced
  coriander root

3 garlic cloves

1½ tablespoons
  chopped galangal

2 lemon grass stalks, chopped

3 hot red chillies

3 tablespoons vegetable oil

1 tablespoon oyster sauce

1 tablespoon light soy sauce

1 teaspoon sugar

1 teaspoon black
  peppercorns, crushed

150g (5oz) squid, cut into
  bite-sized pieces

5 prawns, shelled, deveined
  and heads removed,
  but with tails intact

5 mussels

5 scallops, sliced into bite-
  sized pieces if large

1 tablespoon nam pla
  (Thai fish sauce)

3 pieces of lesser galangal,
  finely sliced

4 baby green peppercorn
  sprigs (available from
  Asian supermarkets),
  roughly chopped

½ onion, sliced

1 tablespoon Chinese rice wine

2 tablespoons water or stock

TO SERVE

Sweet basil leaves

Steamed jasmine rice

Pad Cha in Thai refers to the practice of making your wok so hot that when you add the ingredients, they literally explode. That's what makes this dish so tasty. The flavours, especially the chilli, suddenly explode.

Using a mortar and pestle or a food processor, pound or blitz the coriander root, garlic, chopped galangal, lemon grass and chillies into a paste.

Heat the oil in a wok set over a medium heat. Stir-fry the paste you have made for a few seconds until it is fragrant, then stir in the oyster sauce, soy sauce, sugar and black peppercorns. Add the squid, prawns, mussels and scallops, tossing to combine. Season with the fish sauce, then add the lesser galangal, green peppercorns and onion and combine well. Pour in the Chinese rice wine and measurement water. Cook over a medium heat for a few minutes until everything is cooked through.

Garnish with sweet basil leaves and serve hot with jasmine rice.

STIR-FRIED MUSSELS WITH BASIL LEAVES

SERVES 2

1kg (2lb) mussels

3 garlic cloves

2–3 red spur chillies

2 tablespoons vegetable oil

2 tablespoons roasted chilli paste (available from Asian supermarkets)

I tablespoon granulated sugar

I tablespoon oyster sauce

I tablespoon light soy sauce

I teaspoon nam pla (Thai fish sauce)

I tablespoon chicken stock

Large handful of holy basil leaves

Steamed rice, to serve

I grew up in the mountains, so I didn't eat mussels until I was 12, when my uncle brought some back from the city. Holy basil grows like a weed in Thailand, so we pick large bunches of it and stir-fry it with the mussels – for us, the two just go together!

Check that all the mussels are closed. Gently tap any that aren't, and discard them if they do not close. Clean the mussels in a bowl of water, discarding the beards, then set aside.

Pound the garlic and chillies together using a mortar and pestle.

Heat the oil in a wok set over a high heat, then stir-fry the garlic and chilli mixture until golden brown. Add the roasted chilli paste, stir well, then mix in the mussels. Add the sugar, oyster sauce, soy sauce, fish sauce and chicken stock. Stir-fry for 2 minutes or until the mussels are cooked. Stir in the basil leaves and remove from the heat. Discard any mussels that have not opened up. Serve with rice.

STIR-FRIED ASPARAGUS WITH PRAWNS

SERVES 2

10 asparagus spears

2 tablespoons vegetable oil

2 garlic cloves, chopped

6 prawns (about 40g/1¾oz each), shelled, deveined and heads removed, but with tails intact

1 tablespoon oyster sauce

1 tablespoon light soy sauce

1 teaspoon nam pla (Thai fish sauce)

1 teaspoon granulated sugar

3 tablespoons water or chicken stock

Pinch of white pepper

Steamed rice, to serve

My home town in the north of Thailand is considered cold. Sometimes, the temperature dips as low as 20°C (68°F), which is low enough to make a Thai shiver! It's also just the right temperature to grow asparagus, which thrives in the tropical rain. It's a wonderfully crunchy, refreshing vegetable. I can't remember when I started eating this dish, but I know it came from my mum and began with asparagus simply stir-fried with garlic and oil. Adding the prawns makes for a more substantial dish.

Trim the woody ends off the asparagus, then slice the spears diagonally into pieces, about 6cm (2½ inches) long.

Heat the oil in a wok set over a medium heat and stir-fry the garlic for about 10 seconds until it is almost golden brown. Add the prawns and stir, then add the asparagus and toss to mix well. Stir-fry for about 30 seconds, then add the oyster sauce, light soy sauce, fish sauce and sugar. Increase the heat to high and add the water or stock. Stir-fry for about 2 minutes until the prawns are cooked, then take the pan off the heat.

Spoon into serving dishes, sprinkle with the white pepper and serve with steamed rice.

STIR-FRIED PRAWNS WITH CHILLIES

SERVES 2

3 tablespoons vegetable oil

2 garlic cloves, chopped

10 medium prawns, shelled, deveined and heads removed

1 tablespoon light soy sauce

1 tablespoon oyster sauce

1 teaspoon nam pla (Thai fish sauce)

1 teaspoon granulated sugar

3 small red bird's eye chillies, sliced

1 orange baby pepper, sliced

1 red romano pepper, sliced

20 dried black peppercorns

Pinch of ground white pepper

2 lime leaves, sliced

1 sprig of coriander, leaves roughly chopped

This is the type of traditional Thai street food that I am accustomed to. Although this dish is usually made with pork, I decided on prawns because they were abundant in Hong Kong. The sauce relies on the black pepper, so be generous with it.

Heat the oil in a wok set over a medium heat. When hot, add the garlic and prawns and stir-fry until the prawns are just about cooked. Add the soy sauce, oyster sauce, fish sauce and sugar, then stir in the chillies and peppers and stir-fry for a couple of minutes.

Continue to stir-fry as you add the black peppercorns, ground white pepper and lime leaves. Remove from the heat, stir in the coriander and serve immediately.

SPICY STIR-FRIED COD FISH

SERVES 2

3 garlic cloves

5 red spur chillies, sliced

2 tablespoons vegetable oil

350g (11½oz) line-caught cod
   fillet, cut into large chunks

1 tablespoon oyster sauce

1 tablespoon dark soy sauce

1 teaspoon granulated sugar

1 teaspoon nam pla
   (Thai fish sauce)

1 tablespoon chicken stock

½ teaspoon white pepper

1 Chinese celery stalk,
   roughly chopped

10 basil leaves

4–5 lime leaves

Steamed jasmine rice, to serve

We don't have cod in Thailand, but we do have plenty of catfish. When I lived in Jersey in the late 1990s, the Southeast Asian freshwater catfish was certainly hard to get hold of, so cod became my substitute of choice, as the fluffy yet firm texture of the meat is similar (choose line-caught cod, if you can, or other sustainable fish such as pollock or hake). Catfish, once so common in my life, has now become a delicacy for me.

Pound the garlic and chillies to a paste in a mortar and pestle.

Heat the oil in a wok set over a medium heat. Add the fish and fry it for a couple of minutes on both sides until cooked through. Gently remove from the pan and place on a serving dish.

Add the garlic and chilli paste to the wok and stir-fry for a few seconds. Mix in the oyster sauce, soy sauce, sugar, fish sauce and stock. Add the pepper and Chinese celery, stir in the basil and lime leaves and remove from the heat.

Spoon the sauce over the fish and serve with jasmine rice.

STIR-FRIED CHICKEN WITH CASHEW NUTS

SERVES 4

2 tablespoons vegetable oil

3 garlic cloves, crushed

1 tablespoon roasted chilli paste (available in Asian supermarkets)

500g (1lb) chicken breast, thinly sliced

½ tablespoon nam pla (Thai fish sauce)

1 teaspoon oyster sauce

1 tablespoon light soy sauce

½ teaspoon dark soy sauce

½ tablespoon sugar

1 small onion, sliced

¼ green pepper, chopped

¼ red pepper, chopped

50g (2oz) roasted salted cashew nuts

3 dried spur chillies, cut into 2.5cm (1 inch) pieces and lightly fried

2 tablespoons chicken stock (optional)

2 spring onions, cut into 2.5cm (1 inch) pieces

Steamed rice, to serve

To be honest, this dish isn't Thai at all. It's actually Chinese. But because we often use chicken and cashew nuts in Thailand, we adopted this dish and made it our own by adding Thai spices. It's a sort of hybrid dish and it works very well.

Heat the oil in a wok over a high heat and stir-fry the garlic and chilli paste for a few seconds until fragrant. Add the chicken and stir-fry for 1 minute, then stir in the fish sauce, oyster sauce, light soy sauce, dark soy sauce and sugar. Cook until the chicken is just done.

Add the onion, green and red peppers, cashew nuts and dried chilli to the pan, toss to combine and stir-fry for 1 minute. If the curry is too dry, add a little chicken stock. Stir in the spring onions and remove from the heat.

Spoon into serving dishes and serve with steamed rice.

SPICY STIR-FRIED RED CURRY WITH CHICKEN

SERVES 2–3

3 tablespoons vegetable oil

2 tablespoons Red Curry Paste (see page 202)

500g (1lb) boneless, skinless chicken breast, sliced into bite-sized pieces

2 tablespoons nam pla (Thai fish sauce)

2 tablespoons evaporated milk

2 tablespoons palm sugar

Small handful of sweet basil leaves

2 red spur chillies, diagonally sliced

Steamed rice, to serve

My family is originally from Laos, so much of the food I grew up with wasn't Thai at all. When I was 12, my Laotian uncle married a very traditional Thai woman and she brought this dish that was completely unknown to us to our home town. It was delicious, so I asked my new auntie how she made it. When I started cooking this red curry at my takeaway in Hong Kong, I made it a little creamier than usual to cater for the expat palate. This dish should taste a bit spicy, sweet and salty.

Heat the oil in a wok or saucepan set over a medium heat, add the curry paste and sauté until it is fragrant. Add the chicken and stir-fry until it is cooked through. Stir in the fish sauce, evaporated milk and palm sugar. Add the basil leaves and chillies and toss until everything is combined. Serve immediately with steamed rice.

STIR-FRIED RED CHICKEN CURRY WITH LONG BEANS

SERVES 2

2 tablespoons vegetable oil

2 tablespoons Red Curry Paste (see page 202)

200g (7oz) boneless, skinless chicken breast, cut into bite-sized pieces or strips

250ml (8fl oz) chicken stock

1 tablespoon nam pla (Thai fish sauce)

1 tablespoon granulated sugar

100g (3½oz) yard-long beans (Chinese long beans), sliced into 6cm (2½ inch) pieces

3–4 lime leaves

5–6 Thai basil leaves, plus extra to garnish

2 red chillies, sliced, to garnish

Steamed rice, to serve

When I was around 17 I moved to the main town in my province to study. To earn money while I was away from my parents I worked at my friends' farm. They had a wonderful organic garden full of fresh vegetables and extra crunchy long beans. I combined these with chicken in a curry and the dish was an instant hit!

Heat a wok over a medium heat and add the oil. When it is medium-hot, spoon in the red curry paste and stir-fry for 10 seconds until fragrant. Now add the chicken and stir-fry for 2 minutes. Stir in the chicken stock and fish sauce and, after about 20 seconds, drop in the sugar. Stir-fry for a further 2–3 minutes until the chicken is almost done, then throw in the yard-long beans and stir-fry for another minute. Add the lime and basil leaves, stir-fry for another 30 seconds, then remove the wok from the heat.

Garnish with a few basil leaves and some chilli slices and serve with steamed rice.

STIR-FRIED MINCED CHICKEN WITH RED CURRY

SERVES 2

10 dried large red chilliies

5 garlic cloves, crushed

5 shallots, finely chopped

1 teaspoon shrimp paste (available from Asian supermarkets)

3 tablespoons vegetable oil

350g (11½oz) minced chicken

1½ tablespoons nam pla (Thai fish sauce)

1 tablespoon sugar

400g can chopped tomatoes

Handful of chopped coriander leaves

TO SERVE

Steamed jasmine rice

Sliced raw vegetables, such as spring cabbage, cucumber, yard-long beans or young Thai aubergine

This very northern dish is from the Nan province, which is where my uncle is from. He would make this dish every time I visited him and I'd always look forward to it. I hope you love it as much as I still do. This dish also works well with minced pork instead of chicken.

Using a mortar and pestle or a food processor, pound or blitz the chilli, garlic, shallots and shrimp paste until the mixture has a thick, rough texture. Set aside.

Put the oil into a wok and heat over a high heat until very hot. Add the paste you just made and stir-fry for a few seconds before adding the minced chicken. Stir-fry for about 5 minutes until the chicken is cooked through, adding the fish sauce, sugar and, finally, the tomatoes as you go. Stir in the coriander leaves and serve immediately with rice and sliced, raw vegetables.

STIR-FRIED SPRING VEGETABLES WITH BACON

SERVES 2

2 tablespoons vegetable oil

100g (3½oz) smoked bacon,
 cut into small pieces

2 garlic cloves, finely chopped

2 red bird's eye chillies,
 chopped

2 shallots, finely chopped

1 tablespoon light soy sauce

1 tablespoon oyster sauce

1 teaspoon granulated sugar

½ teaspoon ground
 white pepper

6–7 slices cauliflower

5 asparagus spears, cut into
 2.5cm (1 inch) pieces

150g (5oz) Savoy cabbage, sliced

2 tablespoons chicken stock

2 spring onions, cut into
 2.5cm (1 inch) pieces

Steamed rice, to serve

This is one of my favourite creations. Make sure the vegetables are fresh and crunchy – this is paramount. Get the wok good and hot, chuck in your vegetables and rapidly stir-fry everything. Use a big wok and stir continuously.

....

Set a wok over a medium heat and add the oil. Throw in the bacon and fry it for about 1 minute until cooked through – try not to let it become crispy. Add the garlic, chillies and shallots and stir-fry for 20 seconds.

Pour the soy sauce, oyster sauce and sugar into the wok and stir-fry until the sugar dissolves and the sauce is evenly distributed. Season with the white pepper, then add the vegetables and chicken stock. Rapidly stir-fry for a couple of minutes so that everything is well mixed but the vegetables retain their crunch. Switch off the heat, stir in the spring onions and serve immediately with steamed rice.

CRISPY PORK WITH KRA PROW SAUCE

SERVES 2–3

4 garlic cloves

4 Thai red chillies,
  finely chopped

3 tablespoons vegetable oil

300g (10oz) crispy pork, cubed

1 tablespoon soy sauce

1 tablespoon oyster sauce

4 tablespoons chicken stock

1 teaspoon granulated sugar

100g (3½oz) green beans, cut
  into 5cm (2 inch) pieces

5 Thai basil leaves

Steamed rice, to serve

Pad Kra Prow is a popular Thai dish, so to give it a Hong Kong twist I added crispy pork, which is a very common ingredient in Chinese cooking. You can find it in Chinese supermarkets or make your own at home: buy a slice of pork belly from your local butcher, salt the fat and grill until it is golden brown and crispy. Basically, it's like the crackling you get with your Sunday roast..

Using a pestle and mortar, crush the garlic and chillies into a rough paste.

Heat the oil in a wok set over a medium heat. When hot, add the chilli and garlic paste and stir-fry for a few seconds. Stir in the pork, then add the soy and oyster sauces, stock and sugar. Stir-fry for a further minute, then add the beans. Stir-fry until the pork is heated through. At the last minute, add the basil leaves, stir for 20 seconds, then take off the heat and serve piping hot with steamed rice.

STIR-FRIED BEEF WITH OYSTER SAUCE

SERVES 2

1 teaspoon cornflour

3 tablespoons water

2 tablespoons vegetable oil

2 garlic cloves, finely chopped

200g (7oz) beef tenderloin, sliced into thin, bite-sized strips

1 tablespoon light soy sauce

2 tablespoons oyster sauce

1 tablespoon nam pla (Thai fish sauce)

1 teaspoon granulated sugar

¼ teaspoon crushed black peppercorns

Pinch of white pepper

½ onion, sliced

65g (2½oz) button mushrooms, quartered

½ red pepper, sliced

2 tablespoons stock (optional)

TO SERVE

Bunch of spring onions, cut into 2.5cm (1 inch) pieces

1 red spur chilli, diagonally sliced

Tenderloin beef has always been a favourite of mine, especially when it's cut into thin strips. This dish has its origins with my local butcher in Thailand. He would give us the spare offcuts of beef, which were thinly sliced bits. My mum taught me how to stir-fry the beef with oyster sauce, with a few locally grown vegetables thrown in. It's a simple, healthy dish. It should have a salty taste, with a hint of sweetness.

Mix the cornflour and water in a small bowl and set aside.

Heat the oil in a wok set over a medium heat and stir-fry the garlic until it is almost golden brown. Add the beef to the wok and stir-fry for roughly 2 minutes, until cooked to your liking. Add the soy sauce, oyster sauce, fish sauce, sugar, black peppercorns and white pepper, then stir in the onion, mushrooms and red pepper. Stir-fry for a few minutes until the vegetables are tender. If the sauce seems too dry, add a little stock.

Serve immediately, sprinkled with the spring onion and chilli.

STIR-FRIED BEEF WITH HOLY BASIL

SERVES 2

3 garlic cloves

3 red bird's eye chillies

2 tablespoons vegetable oil

200g (7oz) beef tenderloin, sliced

1 tablespoon nam pla (Thai fish sauce)

1 tablespoon light soy sauce

½ tablespoon granulated sugar

Pinch of ground white pepper

½ small onion, chopped

¼ red or yellow pepper, sliced

30g (1¼oz) yard-long beans (Chinese long beans), chopped

Large handful of holy or Thai basil leaves

2 lime leaves, chopped

Steamed rice, to serve

This dish is a very common on the streets of Thailand. It's easy to make and tastes great. We sometimes call it 'no idea' because if you have no idea what to order in a Thai restaurant, you often just order this! It's widely available and so good that you don't even have to think about it. Whenever you cook this dish, you'll be one of millions of people enjoying it that day. It should be spicy and salty, with a hint of sweetness.

Using a mortar and pestle or a food processor, pound or blitz the chillies and garlic to a paste.

Heat the oil in a wok set over a medium heat and fry the chilli and garlic paste until golden brown.

Add the beef and stir in the fish sauce, light soy sauce, sugar and white pepper. Toss to mix well, then stir-fry for roughly 2 minutes until the beef is cooked.

Add the onion, pepper and long beans, cook for 30 seconds, then mix in the sweet basil and lime leaves. Remove from the heat and serve at once with steamed rice.

STIR-FRIED BEEF WITH FRESH GREEN PEPPERCORNS

SERVES 2

4 red chillies

2 garlic cloves

2cm (1 inch) piece of galangal, peeled and minced

4 fresh green peppercorn sprigs (available from Asian supermarkets), cut into pieces

1 tablespoon vegetable oil

300g (10oz) beef sirloin, sliced

1 tablespoon chicken stock

1 teaspoon nam pla (Thai fish sauce)

1 tablespoon soy sauce

1 tablespoon oyster sauce

4 lime leaves, shredded

1 teaspoon sugar

1 red spur chilli, sliced, to garnish

Steamed rice, to serve

My uncle (whose name is hard to write in English) was an avid hunter of deer, boar, snakes … you get the picture. If you haven't smelt a wild boar, well, its stench is otherworldly, so to mask the pungent waft it would bring into our home, we'd cook it with a significant quantity of herbs and spices. But be warned – the concoction used with beef here has an even stronger smell than wild boar, but is considerably more appealing!

Pound the chillies, garlic, galangal and peppercorns to a paste using a pestle and mortar. Set aside.

Set a wok over a high heat and add the oil. When hot, add the beef and stir-fry for a few seconds, then add the chicken stock, fish sauce, soy sauce, oyster sauce, lime leaves and sugar and stir-fry for about 2 minutes until the beef is cooked through.

Add the pounded chilli mixture and stir-fry for a few seconds until fragrant. Garnish with the sliced spur chilli and serve with steamed rice.

STIR-FRIED VENISON WITH BLACK PEPPER SAUCE

SERVES 2

3 garlic cloves

2 red spur chillies

2 tablespoons vegetable oil

250g (8oz) venison, cut into bite-sized pieces

1 tablespoon oyster sauce

1½ tablespoon nam pla (Thai fish sauce)

1 tablespoon light soy sauce

1 teaspoon granulated sugar

1 teaspoon Chinese rice wine (available from Asian supermarkets)

1 teaspoon ground black peppercorns

1 onion, sliced

¼ red pepper, sliced

¼ green pepper, sliced

¼ yellow pepper, sliced

4 spring onions, cut into 2.5cm (1 inch) pieces

3 fresh green or black peppercorn sprigs (available from Asian supermarkets), cut into pieces

I was young and living in Thailand when I visited Hong Kong for the first time, and tried beef in black bean sauce. I wanted to replicate the dish back home in Thailand, but instead of black beans, I used fresh black peppercorns. Later, when I opened my takeaway business, I substituted venison for beef. I had thought of using ostrich at first, but that fell through. And anyway, I rather preferred the venison!

Pound the garlic and chillies together using a mortar and pestle.

Heat the oil in a wok over a high heat, add the crushed chilli mixture and stir-fry for 30 seconds until fragrant. Add the venison and cook for a further minute. Add the oyster sauce, fish sauce and soy sauce. Stir in the sugar, Chinese rice wine and black peppercorns. After about 5 minutes, or when the venison is done to your liking, add the onion, sliced peppers, spring onions and fresh peppercorns, tossing well.

Spoon into serving dishes and serve immediately.

GRILLS
& MARINADES

FRIED SEA BREAM WITH
CHILLI SAUCE
132

STEAMED SEA BREAM
WITH RED CURRY PASTE
134

ROASTED CHILLI PASTE
WITH SQUID
136

CHICKEN WINGS
IN FISH SAUCE
139

GRILLED CHICKEN IN
GREEN CURRY MARINADE
141

ROASTED SPRING CHICKEN
WITH THAI HERBS
142

CHICKEN IN PANDAN
LEAF MARINADE
144

MARINATED QUAIL
WITH SPICY
THAI DRESSING
146

GRILLED PORK SKEWERS
IN THAI MARINADE
148

LAMB CHOPS WITH
YELLOW CURRY
151

GRILLED BEEF
WITH RED CURRY
152

GRILLED BEEF
WITH SWEET BASIL
SAUCE AND CHILLI
154

TENDERLOIN
SATAYS
156

TIGER'S TEARS
158

FRIED SEA BREAM WITH CHILLI SAUCE

SERVES 2

Vegetable oil, for shallow frying

1 sea bream, about 250g (8oz), cleaned and gutted

½ small onion, finely chopped

¼ green pepper, finely chopped

¼ yellow pepper, finely chopped

¼ red pepper, finely chopped

1 red spur chilli, finely chopped

2 garlic cloves, finely chopped

1 tablespoon light soy sauce

1½ teaspoons nam pla (Thai fish sauce)

1 tablespoon granulated sugar

5 Thai basil leaves, to garnish

I had never tasted sea bream until I went to Hong Kong, this is true, but as soon as I tasted it, I knew in my mind the dish I was going to conjure up – a new version of a dish I originally made with catfish.

Heat 4 tablespoons of the oil in a large, deep frying pan over a medium heat. Shallow-fry the fish for roughly 3 minutes on each side until it is cooked through and golden brown.

When the fish is almost done, heat a wok over a medium heat and add 2 tablespoons of oil. When hot, add the chopped vegetables, chilli and garlic, then the soy sauce, fish sauce and sugar and stir-fry for 30 seconds.

Place the fish on a plate, top with the vegetables, garnish with basil leaves and serve immediately.

STEAMED SEA BREAM WITH RED CURRY PASTE

SERVES 2

I sea bream, about 250g (8oz), cleaned and gutted

2 tablespoons vegetable oil

3 tablespoons Red Curry Paste (see page 202)

2 tablespoons stock (fish, vegetable or chicken)

2 tablespoons nam pla (Thai fish sauce)

I teaspoon granulated sugar

4cm (I¾ inch) piece of lesser galangal, finely chopped, plus extra to garnish

4 sprigs of Thai basil

TO GARNISH

6 lime leaves, finely chopped

I red spur chilli, finely sliced

Sprig of Thai basil

In the jungle near my home town, there was a deep canal that was full of catfish. We would catch some and cook this dish for our lunch, right there next to the canal, on a portable stone barbecue – a jungle picnic of sorts. I can safely say that I've never had a fish dish so fresh, but these days, when catching my own catfish is not an option, I use sea bream as fresh as I can get. It still tastes wonderful.

Steam the fish for 5 minutes in a steamer set over a high heat.

Meanwhile, heat a wok over a medium heat and add the oil. When hot, add the red curry paste and stir-fry for about a minute until fragrant. Now add the stock, fish sauce, sugar and galangal and stir-fry for about 2 minutes until the sugar dissolves. The sauce should be quite thick. Finally, drop in the sweet basil and turn off the heat.

Put the fish on a serving plate and slowly pour over the stir-fried sauce. Serve immediately, sprinkled with the lime leaves, lesser galangal and chilli, and topped with a basil sprig.

ROASTED CHILLI PASTE WITH SQUID

SERVES 2

400g (13oz) squid, cleaned and split open lengthways

3 tablespoons vegetable oil

2 garlic cloves, minced

2 tablespoons roasted chilli paste (available from Asian supermarkets)

2 tablespoons evaporated milk

1 teaspoon granulated sugar

1 tablespoon light soy sauce

1 teaspoon nam pla (Thai fish sauce)

1 onion, chopped

1 red pepper, chopped

1 green pepper, chopped

1 spring onion, finely chopped

Steamed rice, to serve

I believe that every single Thai person, and I mean literally everyone (even the rare few who are allergic to chillies), loves this dish. Please try it!

Open out the squid, score the inside of the flesh in a diamond pattern, then cut into bite-sized pieces. Set aside.

Heat the oil in a wok set over a low heat. When hot, add the garlic and stir-fry until golden brown. Add the squid to the pan and continue to stir-fry, gradually increasing the heat so that the mixture begins to sizzle.

Stir in the roasted chilli paste, evaporated milk, sugar, soy sauce and fish sauce, then add the onion and peppers and stir-fry for an additional 2 minutes.

Sprinkle over the spring onion, reduce the heat and simmer for another 2 minutes. Serve with rice.

CHICKEN WINGS IN FISH SAUCE

SERVES 2

6 chicken wings

4 tablespoons nam pla (Thai fish sauce)

½ teaspoon ground cumin

Vegetable oil, for deep-frying

2 pandan leaves, chopped

Fried onions, to garnish

Sweet Chilli Sauce (see page 210), to serve

It might sound odd to combine meat and fish, but it's wonderful – also simple and delicious. I believe this is all that needs to be said about this dish!

Mix the chicken wings with the fish sauce and the ground cumin, then leave the mixture in the refrigerator to marinate for at least 1 hour.

Heat the oil in a deep-fat fryer or a wok over a medium heat. When hot, add the pandan leaves and marinated chicken wings. Deep-fry until the wings are golden brown and cooked through and the pandan leaves are crisp. Drain on kitchen paper, scatter over the fried onions and serve immediately with the dipping sauce.

GRILLED CHICKEN IN GREEN CURRY MARINADE

SERVES 2

2 boneless, skinless chicken breasts, about 100g (3½oz) each

FOR THE MARINADE

2 tablespoons Green Curry Paste (see page 203)

2 teaspoons granulated sugar

1 tablespoon nam pla (Thai fish sauce)

1 teaspoon ground cumin

2 tablespoons coconut milk

3 lime leaves, shredded

2 pieces of lesser galangal, about 5cm (2 inches) long, finely chopped

While living on the island of Jersey, I ate a roast dinner every Sunday, as was the norm in many British households. But, of course, I couldn't resist tweaking! Well, I say 'tweaking' but, in reality, I revamped the whole concept of a roast to incorporate the Thai style of cooking. This recipe worked unbelievably well with the usual roast dinner trimmings, especially the roast potatoes. You should definitely try this one Sunday afternoon.

....

Mix all the ingredients for the marinade in a bowl, ensuring they are evenly combined. Firmly rub the marinade over the chicken breasts, ensuring you get it into all the nooks and crannies. Put the breasts into a bowl and leave them in the refrigerator for 1 hour to marinate.

Preheat a griddle pan until very hot, or preheat the oven to 220°C/425°F/Gas Mark 7. If using a griddle, place the chicken in it and cook for about 5 minutes on each side until done. Alternatively, place the chicken breasts in a roasting pan and roast for roughly 10–15 minutes, or until the juices run clear when the meat is pierced with a skewer.

Slice the chicken breasts and serve with traditional roast dinner trimmings of your choice.

ROASTED SPRING CHICKEN WITH THAI HERBS

SERVES 4

3cm (1¼ inch) piece of galangal, sliced

3 lemon grass stalks, finely chopped

6–7 garlic cloves

4 coriander roots, roughly chopped

½ pandan leaf, finely chopped (optional)

4 tablespoons light soy sauce

1 tablespoon oyster sauce

2 tablespoons honey

½ teaspoon ground turmeric

½ teaspoon freshly ground white pepper

2 small spring chickens or poussins, about 500g (1lb) each, cut in half and flattened

Side salad of your choice, to serve

Around 26 years ago I drove from my home town in northern Thailand to Hong Kong via Bangkok. When I was about half-way to Bangkok, in the district of Wichian Buri, I passed a roadside chicken restaurant, a small welcoming wicker shack, and ordered a plate of chicken. I was blown away. The guru of this recipe was an 80-year-old woman who kindly gave it to me. This shack is now a sprawling eatery that serves over 3,000 chickens each day. I'm not surprised.

Using a mortar and pestle or a food processor, pound or blitz the galangal, lemon grass, garlic, coriander and pandan leaf, if using, to a paste. Set the spice mixture aside.

Now make a marinade by combining the soy sauce, oyster sauce, honey, turmeric and white pepper in a large bowl. Stir well.

Place the chicken in the marinade and mix well. Rub the galangal mixture all over the chicken and leave to marinate in the refrigerator for 1 hour or so.

Preheat the oven to 180°C/350°F/Gas Mark 4. Place the marinated chicken in a roasting pan and roast for roughly 40 minutes until golden brown and cooked through. To check for this, the juices should run clear when the flesh is pierced with a skewer. Serve with a side salad.

CHICKEN IN PANDAN LEAF MARINADE

MAKES 10–12 BITE-SIZED PIECES

200g (7oz) boneless, skinless chicken breast, cut into 10–12 chunks

1 tablespoon coriander seeds

3 garlic cloves

20 white peppercorns

1 pandan leaf (available from Asian supermarkets), finely chopped

1 tablepoon sesame oil

2 tablespoons soy sauce

1½ tablespoons oyster sauce

1 tablespoon granulated sugar

3 tablespoons vegetable oil

1 red chilli, sliced, to garnish

FOR THE DIPPING SAUCE

3 tablespoons water

3 tablespoons brown sugar

1 tablespoon dark soy sauce

3 tablespoons light soy sauce

1 tablespoon toasted sesame seeds

When I was 21 years old, I worked for a very small restaurant called Thai Farmer. The best-seller was this dry curry of sorts, with the distinctive taste of pandan leaf. Over the years I've tweaked the recipe a little – it's perfect on a cold winter's day.

....

Place the chicken pieces in a large bowl.

Pound the coriander seeds, garlic, peppercorns and pandan leaf together using a pestle and mortar. Add the mixture to the chicken, followed by the sesame oil, soy sauce, oyster sauce and sugar. Mix well, then leave to marinate in the refrigerator for about 1 hour.

Meanwhile, prepare the dipping sauce. Heat the measurement water in a small saucepan over a low heat, then add the sugar, soy sauces and sesame seeds and stir until the sugar has dissolved. Simmer until the sauce has thickened slightly, then take the pan off the heat and leave to cool.

To cook the chicken, heat the oil in a wok set over a medium heat. One by one, place the pieces of marinated chicken in the pan and fry for about 5 minutes until cooked through and golden brown.

Transfer to a serving plate, garnish with the chilli and serve with the dipping sauce.

MARINATED QUAIL WITH SPICY THAI DRESSING

SERVES 2

4 small quail, plucked
and cleaned

FOR THE MARINADE

2 lemon grass stalks,
finely chopped

3 shallots, chopped

4 garlic cloves, finely chopped

3 coriander roots, chopped

1 teaspoon salt

FOR THE DIPPING SAUCE

2 tablespoons nam pla
(Thai fish sauce)

2 tablespoons lime juice

1 tablespoon chilli powder

1 spring onion, chopped

1 teaspoon roasted rice
(available in Asian
supermarkets or see
page 13), crushed

TO SERVE

Slices of fresh cucumber
and red pepper

Chinese cabbage or iceberg
lettuce, chilled

Thai basil leaves

My best friend, Sayo, is a cosmopolitan woman who is very much accustomed to Western cuisine. One day she decided to show off her Thai culinary skills to me, which I realized I had underestimated as soon as I took the first bite of this dish – it is amazing! Thank you, Sayo, for giving me this recipe. I advise readers not to underestimate this dish as I did or you might miss out on something very special.

Spatchcock the quails by cutting them through the underside, then flattening them out lengthways. Set aside.

Make the marinade. Use a mortar and pestle to crush the lemon grass, shallots, garlic, coriander roots and salt to a thoroughly mixed rough paste. Put this mixture in a bowl with the quail and use it to coat the meat. Leave the quail in the refrigerator to marinate for at least 1 hour.

Preheat the oven to 180°C/350°F/Gas Mark 4.

Put the marinated quail into a roasting pan and place it in the oven for 45 minutes.

While the quail is cooking, make the dip. Combine the fish sauce, lime juice, chilli powder and chopped spring onion in a bowl. Decant the mixture into a sauce dish and top with the roasted rice.

Once the quail is cooked, leave it to stand for a couple of minutes, then cut into medium-sized pieces if you wish. Serve the quail with the dipping sauce and the salad.

GRILLED PORK SKEWERS IN THAI MARINADE

MAKES 8 SKEWERS

500g (1lb) boneless
    pork tenderloin, cut
    into thin slices

FOR THE MARINADE:

3 coriander roots,
    roughly chopped

20 white peppercorns

4–5 garlic cloves

I teaspoon coriander seeds

5 tablespoons oyster sauce

5 tablespoons soy sauce

5 tablespoons nam pla
    (Thai fish sauce)

2 tablespoons sugar

I tablespoon honey

3 tablespoons cornflour

5 tablespoons vegetable oil

sticky rice, to serve

FOR THE DIPPING SAUCE

2 tablespoons lime juice

I tablespoon nam pla
    (Thai fish sauce)

I red chilli, finely chopped

In my family, these skewers would be made to give to the kids to eat while they walk to school – breakfast with a side order of sticky rice. They are such a part of my childhood, I just had to include the recipe in this book. They are super-simple to make and taste delicious. You can cook them in a griddle pan or under a grill, but they're also great for the barbecue.

Pound the garlic, peppercorns, coriander roots and coriander seeds using a mortar and pestle. Add the oyster sauce, soy sauce, fish sauce, sugar, honey, cornflour and vegetable oil and mix well. Add the pork slices, ensure they are well coated in the mixture, then marinate in the refrigerator for at least I hour.

Meanwhile, place 8 wooden skewers in water and leave them to soak.

Preheat a grill or griddle pan until very hot. Meanwhile, thread the marinated pork on to skewers (2 or 3 slices per skewer). Grill or griddle the skewers for I–2 minutes on each side, or until cooked through.

Mix together the ingredients for the dipping sauce. Serve the skewers with sticky rice and the dipping sauce.

LAMB CHOPS WITH YELLOW CURRY

SERVES 2

2 tablespoons vegetable oil

1½ tablespoons yellow curry paste (see page 202)

250ml (8fl oz) coconut milk

1 tablespoon nam pla (Thai fish sauce)

1 teaspoon palm sugar

Pinch of salt

4 lamb chops, about 100g (3½oz) each

TO SERVE

Handful of fresh coriander leaves

1 red chilli, sliced

Thai people don't usually eat lamb; its aroma is unfamiliar, so it is something of a rarity in Thai food. I love it, though. Since it's a common ingredient in Britain, I decided to try a twist on a yellow curry to serve with lamb chops, so this is a unique dish that you won't find anywhere else. I have to say, I think it tastes fab. The trick with this curry is to keep its consistency thick, so don't add any water.

To make the curry sauce, put the oil in a pan over a medium heat, add the yellow curry paste and cook for about 30 seconds until the oil splits and rises to the surface. Add the coconut milk, fish sauce, palm sugar and salt and cook for 5 minutes. The curry sauce should be quite thick and taste slightly salty. When the mixture comes to the boil, the curry is ready to serve.

Meanwhile, preheat a grill or griddle and cook the lamb chops for about 3 minutes on each side or until done to your liking. Transfer to a warm plate and keep warm in a low oven until ready to serve.

Put the lamb on a serving plate and serve the curry sauce on the side, or pour it over the meat if you prefer. Garnish with coriander leaves and sliced chillies.

GRILLED BEEF WITH RED CURRY

SERVES 2

2 tablespoons vegetable oil

3 tablespoons Red Curry Paste (see page 202)

200ml (7fl oz) coconut milk

2 tablespoons nam pla (Thai fish sauce)

1 tablespoon palm sugar

200g (7oz) canned pineapple pieces in juice

100g (3½oz) French beans

½ green pepper, chopped

½ red pepper, chopped

200ml (7fl oz) chicken stock (optional)

2 sirloin steaks, weighing 250g (8oz) in total

Steamed rice, to serve

TO GARNISH

5 lime leaves, chopped

5–6 Thai basil leaves

In Thailand it's hard to find cooked meat that hasn't been grilled. Microwaves are uncommon and an open grill is the norm – and so it should be, in my opinion! This dish relies on the quality of the meat, so I recommend you try your local butcher rather than rely on a supermarket.

Pour the oil into a deep saucepan and heat until very hot. Spoon in the red curry paste and fry for 20 seconds, then add the coconut milk and cook, stirring constantly, until the red oil rises to the top.

Add the fish sauce, palm sugar, pineapple pieces and their juice, and cook, stirring constantly, for 2 minutes. Add the French beans, green and red peppers and cook for 3–5 minutes until cooked through. If the curry is too dry for your liking, add 200ml (7fl oz) chicken stock at the end and heat through.

Meanwhile, preheat the grill to medium-hot. Cook the steaks under it for 2 minutes on each side if you want them medium rare – use this timing as a guide and grill the steaks for more or less time so that they are cooked to your liking.

Divide the curry between 2 serving plates, garnish with the lime and basil leaves and serve immediately with the beef and some steamed rice.

GRILLED BEEF WITH SWEET BASIL SAUCE AND CHILLI

SERVES 2

3 garlic cloves

3 red spur chillies

2 teaspoons soy sauce

I teaspoon brown sugar

I teaspoon crushed
    black peppercorns

I teaspoon nam pla
    (Thai fish sauce)

2 tablespoons vegetable oil

Handful of Thai basil leaves

250g (8oz) beef tenderloin steak

Rice or fresh vegetables,
    to serve

This dish reminds me of the late 1980s, but I don't have any nostalgic memories of big hair, shoulder pads and excess. I associate this era with 'freedom', by which I mean the great outdoors. In other words, we didn't have a refrigerator. The best way to preserve meat, other than salting it, was to grill and dry it. After that, it would keep for days. In order to finish it off towards the end of its freshness, we would make this dish. It was always my favourite of all the concoctions that had preceeded it. The spicy, sweet and salty notes complement the beef's subtle flavour perfectly.

Pound the garlic and chilli together using a mortar and pestle and set aside.

In a small bowl, mix the soy sauce, brown sugar, peppercorns and fish sauce and set aside.

Place a wok over a high heat and pour in the oil. Add the garlic and chilli mixture and stir-fry for a few seconds, then pour in soy sauce mixture. Add the basil leaves, mix everything together thoroughly, then take off the heat.

Heat a griddle pan over a medium heat, add the beef and cook until it is done to your liking (about 2 minutes on each side will make it medium-rare).

Cut the steak into pieces and transfer to a serving plate. Pour over the sauce and serve immediately with rice or fresh vegetables.

TENDERLOIN SATAYS

SERVES 2–3

500g (1lb) beef tenderloin,
    cut into thin strips

FOR THE MARINADE

3 lemon grass stalks, chopped

4 pandan leaves
    (available from Asian
    supermarkets), chopped

3 tablespoons chopped galangal

150ml (¼ pint) coconut milk

150g (5oz) pineapple chunks

1 teaspoon turmeric

2 teaspoons curry powder

1 tablespoon nam pla
    (Thai fish sauce)

3 tablespoons vegetable oil

1 tablespoon ground coriander

1 tablespoon caraway seeds

2 tablespoons sugar

1 tablespoon oyster sauce

1 tablespoon light soy sauce

FOR THE PEANUT SAUCE

250ml (8fl oz) coconut milk

½ tablespoon Red Curry
    Paste (see page 202)

½ tablespoon Massaman
    Curry Paste (see page 203)

2 tablespoons palm sugar

1 tablespoon nam pla
    (Thai fish sauce)

100ml (3½fl oz) tamarind paste

150g (5oz) crushed
    roasted peanuts

In Thailand, beef is pretty tough, so we have to marinate it for a long time to make it tender. This marinade recipe is a good one to note as it will tenderize almost any meat if left for long enough. For beef, I suggest a minimum of an hour.

Put all marinade ingredients into a blender and blitz to a smooth paste, or pound them in a pestle and mortar. Transfer the mixture to a bowl. Add the beef strips and mix well. Marinate in the refrigerator for about 2 hours. Meanwhile, place 6-9 wooden skewers in water and leave to soak.

To make the peanut sauce, bring the coconut milk to the boil in a small saucepan and cook until the oil comes to the surface. Stir in the curry pastes and cook for about 30 seconds, then add the palm sugar, fish sauce, tamarind sauce and the roasted peanuts. Reduce the heat to low and cook, stirring continuously, until the mixture has thickened a little and has a smooth consistency.

Preheat a grill or griddle pan until very hot. Thread the beef strips on to the skewers, then cook for about 2 minutes on each side or until done to your liking. Serve hot with the peanut sauce.

TIGER'S TEARS

SERVES 2

I teaspoon soy sauce

I coriander root, finely chopped

I teaspoon ground white pepper

I teaspoon oyster sauce

200g (Ilb) beef steak

FOR THE DIPPING SAUCE

2 tablespoons nam pla
   (Thai fish sauce)

3 tablespoons lime juice

I small shallot, finely chopped

I teaspoon roasted rice
   (available from Asian
   supermarkets or see page 13)

I teaspoon chili powder

I teaspoon finely chopped
   fresh coriander leaves

I will explain why we call this dish Tiger's Tears. You know when you grill beef on a barbecue and the fat or water drips on to the charcoal and makes a hissing sound? Well, the drops of water represent the tears and the hissing represents the tiger. My dad is absolutely crazy about grilled beef and this is his recipe. It goes so well with Thai whisky.

Mix the soy sauce, coriander root, pepper and oyster sauce in a bowl. Add the beef and mix well. Marinate in the refrigerator for I hour.

Meanwhile, put all the ingredients for the dipping sauce into a bowl and mix well. Transfer to a serving bowl.

Preheat a griddle pan until very hot. Add the beef and grill for about 2–3 minutes, turning once, until cooked to your liking. Slice and serve the beef with the dipping sauce.

NOODLES
& RICE

RICE NOODLES WITH CHICKPEA RED CURRY SAUCE

SERVES 2

150g (5oz) rice vermicelli

400ml (14fl oz) coconut milk

2 tablespoons Red Curry Paste (see page 202)

3 lime leaves, torn

125g (4oz) canned chickpeas (drained weight – about half a can)

8cm (3¼ inch) piece of lesser galangal

1½ tablespoons palm sugar

2 tablespoons tamarind pulp

2 tablespoons nam pla (Thai fish sauce)

TO SERVE

2 sweet basil sprigs

Roasted dried chillies (available from Asian supermarkets)

Finely shredded cabbage

Thinly sliced cucumber

Handful of bean sprouts

This one goes back to when I was around seven years old. You might wonder how I remember a recipe from such a long time ago. Well, this top-class dish is so delicious, I can recall the flavour of it right now: there's no way I would forget this recipe.

Put the rice noodles in large pan of boiling water, then reduce the heat and simmer for 10 minutes until they are soft. Drain and set aside.

Meanwhile, set a saucepan over a medium heat and add half the coconut milk. Cook for 2 minutes until the oil in the coconut milk starts spitting, then stir in the curry paste and cook for a further 3 minutes. Add the remaining coconut milk and the lime leaves and cook for 2 minutes more.

Meanwhile, roughly crush the chickpeas using a mortar and pestle, then set aside. Pound the galangal using the mortar and pestle.

Soak the tamarind pulp in 4 tablespoons of warm water for a few minutes, then stir until it becomes a thick liquid.

Add the crushed chickpeas, galangal and palm sugar to the pan, then stir in the tamarind and the fish sauce. Simmer for 10 minutes.

Plate up the noodles as you would spaghetti. Garnish each plate with a sprig of basil, some dried chillies and plenty of bean sprouts and fresh green vegetables. Serve the curry sauce in a small side dish, or pour the sauce over the noodles and serve immediately.

DRY NOODLES WITH FRESH TOFU

SERVES 2

300g (10oz) egg noodles
  or rice vermicelli

150g (5oz) bean sprouts

1 tablespoon vegetable oil

2 garlic cloves, finely chopped

200g (7oz) soft tofu,
  cut into chunks

1 tablespoon nam pla
  (Thai fish sauce)

½ teaspoon dark soy sauce

1 tablespoon light soy sauce

1 teaspoon granulated sugar

2 tablespoons roasted
  peanuts, crushed

1 teaspoon dried chilli flakes

1 spring onion, finely sliced

1 sprig of coriander,
  leaves chopped

1 lime, halved

Fish and chips, wrapped up in newspaper, with a dash of salt and vinegar are synonymous with the UK. In Thailand, we wrap this noodle dish in newspaper. It isn't as famous as fish and chips are in the UK, but it is just a tasty, if not more so – please don't feel insulted if you are British! In this dish, the noodles are not served in soup, which is why they are 'dry'.

Bring a wok or saucepan of water to the boil and add the noodles and bean sprouts. Boil for 30 seconds, then drain and put them on a plate.

Meanwhile, heat the oil in small saucepan over a high heat, add the garlic and cook, stirring continuously, until it is golden brown. Remove from the pan and set aside.

Put the tofu and fried garlic on top of the bean sprouts and noodles, then add the fish sauce, soy sauces and sugar and mix well to combine. Sprinkle with the crushed peanuts and dried chill. Top with the spring onion and coriander and serve with lime wedges to squeeze over.

STIR-FRIED EGG NOODLES

SERVES 2

50g (2oz) dried perfume (huong) mushrooms

3 tablespoons vegetable oil

1 egg, beaten

2 garlic cloves, chopped

200g (7oz) fresh egg noodles

2 tablespoons sugar

1 tablespoon light soy sauce

1 tablespoon oyster sauce

20g (¾oz) bean sprouts

2 spring onions, chopped

1 teaspoon dark soy sauce

Pinch of white pepper

Jay season, an annual event in Thailand, is a kind of homage to vegetarians; it is linked to Buddhism – Buddhist monks do not eat meat. During the month of July we hold a nationwide vegetarian food festival and this dish features prominently.

Soak the mushrooms in a little hot water for a few minutes until soft. Drain and slice them, then set aside.

Place a wok over a medium heat. Add the oil and, when hot, add the egg, stirring constantly. Add the garlic and stir-fry until it is golden brown.

Add the noodles and mix well. After a few seconds, add the sugar, light soy sauce, oyster sauce and mushrooms and stir-fry until everything is well combined. Finally, add the bean sprouts and spring onions and season with the dark soy sauce.

Tip the noodles on to 2 serving plates and sprinkle with the white pepper. Serve immediately.

PAD THAI PRAWN

Pad Thai is probably the most famous of all Thai noodle dishes. It's always a safe bet to serve this dish because everybody loves it, even the fussiest of eaters. Deliciously pungent tamarind is the key ingredient in this dish.

....

SERVES 2

4 eggs, beaten

300g (10oz) rice noodles, soaked in warm water for 20 minutes, then drained

8–10 prawns, shelled, deveined and heads removed

2 tablespoons dried turnip (available from Asian supermarkets)

2 handfuls of bean sprouts

Chilli powder, to taste (optional)

Bunch of Chinese chives or 2 spring onions, chopped

4 tablespoons roasted peanuts, crushed

Lime wedges, to serve

FOR THE PAD THAI SAUCE

3 tablespoons tamarind pulp

3 tablespoons vegetable oil

3 shallots, chopped

2 tablespoons palm sugar

1 tablespoon nam pla (Thai fish sauce)

First make the Pad Thai sauce. Soak the tamarind pulp in 6 tablespoons of warm water, then stir until it becomes a thick liquid.

Heat 2 tablespoons of the oil in a wok, add the shallots and stir-fry until almost golden brown. Carefully add the tamarind (in case it spits) and cook for 1 minute to reduce slightly.

Add the palm sugar, stirring to break it up, then stir in the fish sauce and continue to cook over a high heat for 1 minute until it has thickened slightly. Transfer the Pad Thai sauce to a bowl and set aside. This recipe makes enough sauce for about 4 servings, so store any leftover Pad Thai sauce in an airtight container and use within 4 weeks.

Now prepare the noodles. Scramble the beaten eggs in a hot wok with the remaining oil, then add the noodles and stir-fry until the egg breaks up and the noodles are soft. Add the prawns and dried turnip and stir-fry until the prawns are nearly cooked. Mix in 8 tablespoons of the reserved Pad Thai sauce and continue to stir-fry until the noodles take on a nice golden brown colour. Add the bean sprouts, chilli powder (if using), Chinese chives and crushed peanuts and keep stir-frying for another 2 minutes.

Transfer the noodles to 2 serving plates and serve immediately with lime wedges.

SEAFOOD IN THAI GRAVY WITH BEETROOT

SERVES 2

1 tablespoon vegetable oil

150g (5oz) flat rice noodles

1 teaspoon dark soy sauce

2 tablespoons vegetable oil

3 garlic cloves, chopped

4 prawns, peeled and deveined

20g (¾oz) squid, scored with a diamond pattern and chopped

20g (¾oz) scallops, sliced into bite-sized pieces

20g (¾oz) mussels, cleaned and debearded

1 teaspoon yellow bean paste

2 tablespoons light soy sauce

1 tablespoon oyster sauce

1 tablespoon brown sugar

150ml (¼ pint) chicken stock

1 tablespoon cornflour

100g (3½oz) mixed vegetables (such as spring cabbage, broccoli, carrots and mangetout), chopped

1 cooked beetroot, thinly sliced

Pinch of white pepper

Until I moved to Jersey, I had never seen a beetroot before in my life. I was curious to discover what it would go with, so I bought one and stir-fried it in some Thai gravy. It tasted amazing: the beetroot's natural deep red colour and earthy flavour melded so well with the essence of the dish that I instantly fell in love with this marvellous vegetable.

Set a wok over a medium heat and add the oil. When hot, throw in the noodles and stir-fry for 20 seconds. Add the dark soy sauce and stir-fry for 3 minutes, then take the pan off the heat and set aside.

Heat another wok or deep frying pan and add the oil. When hot, add the garlic and stir-fry until golden brown. Chuck in the seafood, then add the yellow bean paste, light soy sauce, oyster sauce and sugar and cook, stirring continuously. When you are sure the seafood is cooked through, mix the chicken stock and cornflour in a small bowl and pour the mixture into the pan and stir until slightly thickened. Add the mixed vegetables and beetroot and cook briefly – you want them all to retain some crunch.

To serve, divide the noodle mixture between 2 plates, pour the gravy over them and season with the white pepper. Serve immediately.

SPICY SEAFOOD SPAGHETTI

SERVES 1

150g (5oz) spaghetti

1 squid, cleaned and slit
    open lengthways

2 teaspoons vegetable oil

1 tablespoon chopped garlic

1 tablespoon chopped red chilli

3 mussels, cleaned
    and debearded

2 prawns, peeled and deveined

3 scallops

½ onion, chopped

½ red pepper, chopped

½ green pepper, chopped

2 teaspoons oyster sauce

1 tablespoon dark soy sauce

1 teaspoon granulated sugar

Handful of sweet basil leaves

Salt

Legend has it that Marco Polo discovered noodles when travelling in China. He tried to replicate them when he got back to Italy, but used wheat instead of rice flour, and so spaghetti was born. There's also a legend about the origin of this dish. Khee Meow means 'drunk' in Thai, and it was rumoured that only drunkards would cook and eat this dish. It's extremely spicy, so is good for a hangover – the idea is that the power of the chilli overwhelms the pain of the morning after!

Bring a saucepan of salted water to a rolling boil and add the spaghetti. Cook according to the packet instructions. Drain and set aside.

Meanwhile, open out the squid, score the inside in a diamond pattern, then chop into bite-sized pieces.

Heat the oil in a wok and sauté the garlic and chilli until fragrant.

Add all the seafood and stir-fry for 2 minutes over a high heat.

Tip in the cooked spaghetti, then the onion and peppers and stir-fry for another minute. Add all the seasonings to the wok and stir-fry for another 2 minutes over a high heat to allow the flavours to mingle.

Stir in the sweet basil, spoon the spaghetti on to a plate and serve immediately.

THAI SPAGHETTI SAUCE WITH CRAB

SERVES 2

250g (8oz) spaghetti

5 tablespoons olive oil

3 large garlic cloves, chopped

2 red spur chillies, chopped

3 shallots, chopped

3–4 tablespoons cooked crab
  meat and/or crab roe

2 fresh crab legs, cooked

Pinch of salt

Pinch of black pepper

Handful of fresh
  coriander, chopped

TO GARNISH

1 red chilli, sliced

Sprigs of sweet basil

Hong Kong is famous for crispy pork and roast duck, and also for the hairy crab or mitten crab, known for its tasty roe that would often appear in my dishes. When I was living in Hong Kong, I developed a taste for Italian food and began to substitute spaghetti for rice noodles in Thai dishes. This dish is one of my favourites and has a fantastic depth of flavour, whichever type of crab you use – the subtle taste of spaghetti is the cherry on top!

Bring a saucepan of salted water to a rolling boil and add the spaghetti. Cook according to the packet instructions.

When the pasta has been cooking for 5 minutes, heat the oil in a wok over a high heat. Add the garlic, chillies and shallots and stir-fry for around 10 seconds. Add the crab meat and legs and stir-fry for another 2 minutes, throwing in the salt and pepper as you go do so. Now reduce the heat to low and stir in the chopped coriander.

Drain the spaghetti, put it into a large bowl and add the crab. Mix well, then serve immediately, garnished with the sliced chilli and sweet basil.

PINEAPPLE FRIED RICE

SERVES 2

1 small pineapple

2 tablespoons vegetable oil

1 teaspoon butter

3 garlic cloves, chopped

3 mussels, cleaned
and debearded

2 prawns, shelled and deveined

3 scallops, sliced into bite-
sized pieces if large

250g (8oz) squid, scored
with a diamond pattern
and chopped

1 tablespoon light soy sauce

1 tablespoon nam pla
(Thai fish sauce)

1 teaspoon granulated sugar

1 teaspoon ground turmeric

¼ red pepper, finely chopped

¼ green pepper, finely chopped

1 tablespoon diced onion

300g (10oz) cooked jasmine rice

Fresh coriander leaves,
to garnish

In 1988 I was 18 years old and living in Hong Kong, working as a nanny and with a part-time job at a friend's restaurant. This is when I really came into my own as a cook. I absorbed many influences and learned a lot of recipes. This is one of the dishes my friend taught me. It's great as a main course, but also makes an exceptional side dish to a seafood curry if you don't add the seafood to the rice.

Cut a thick lengthways slice from one side of the pineapple. Using a small, sharp knife, hollow out the pineapple and dice the flesh. You will need 65g (2½oz) diced pineapple for this recipe, so save the rest to eat later.

Heat the oil and butter in wok, add the garlic and stir-fry until it starts to turn golden brown, then add the seafood. Cook for 2 minutes or until done, then add the soy sauce, fish sauce, sugar and turmeric and stir-fry for a further minute. Add the red and green pepper, onion and diced pineapple and stir-fry for 1 minute.

Finally, add the cooked rice, stirring and mixing well. Stir-fry until everything is heated through.

Spoon the mixture into the hollowed-out pineapple and serve sprinkled with coriander leaves.

SHRIMP FRIED RICE

SERVES 2

2 tablespoons vegetable oil

I teaspoon chopped garlic

200g (7oz) peeled prawns

I tablespoon soy sauce

I tablespoon oyster sauce

I teaspoon nam pla
(Thai fish sauce)

Pinch of ground white pepper

I carrot, sliced diagonally

50g (2oz) button
mushrooms, sliced

½ onion, sliced

2 spring onions, sliced

275g (9oz) cooked rice
(leftovers are fine)

I tablespoon water

Juice of ½ lime

Sliced spring onion, to garnish

Fried rice is basic Thai Cuisine, wonderful and simple – you will probably find it at every single food stall in Thailand. No matter where you are, this staple dish is always served with a squeeze of lime juice and some young spring onions sprinkled over the top. The trick is to eat a spoonful of rice and then quickly eat some spring onion afterwards – that gives the palate a subtle kick, ready for your next spoonful.

Heat the oil in a wok set over a high heat. When hot, add the garlic and stir-fry for a few seconds until fragant. Add the prawns, then pour in the soy sauce, oyster sauce and fish sauce and season with the pepper. Add the carrot, mushrooms, onions and spring onions and stir-fry for about 2 minutes until everything is cooked.

Add the cooked rice and stir-fry for about I minute to heat through. Stir in the water, squeeze over some lime juice and serve immediately, garnished with spring onion slices.

STIR-FRIED THICK FLAT NOODLES

SERVES 2

2 tablespoons vegetable oil

1 tablespoon crushed garlic

1 egg, beaten

125g (4oz) sirloin steak, thinly sliced

150g (5oz) thick, flat fresh rice noodles

1 tablespoon oyster sauce

1 tablespoon dark soy sauce

Pinch of white pepper

½ tablespoon nam pla (Thai fish sauce)

1 teaspoon granulated sugar

Large handful of Chinese kale, roughly chopped

Handful of mangetout

Small handful of sliced spring cabbage

Handful of bean sprouts

Friday is market day in my home town. It's the main attraction of the week, and everybody looks forward to it. This basic, healthy and very tasty dish was always sold at the food stalls. It's like a sister dish to Pad Thai, with a pinch of white pepper that adds a distinctive taste to the saltiness of the soy and oyster sauces.

Heat the oil in a wok over a medium heat. When hot, stir-fry the garlic until fragrant. Pour in the egg and stir-fry until it turns a milky orange colour. Add the beef and stir-fry for about 1 minute until it is cooked through.

Add the noodles and stir well to combine. Mix in the oyster sauce and soy sauce and stir-fry for 1 minute. Season with the pepper, fish sauce and sugar. Add all the vegetables, stir-fry for a few moments, making sure that everything is well combined.

Spoon on to 2 serving plates and serve immediately.

BASIL-FRIED PORK VERMICELLI

SERVES 2

150g (5oz) rice vermicelli

2 tablespoons vegetable oil

1 teaspoon chopped garlic

250g (8oz) minced pork

2 tablepoons soy sauce

1 teaspoon nam pla
   (Thai fish sauce)

1 tablespoon sugar

1 pinch of ground white pepper

Handful of Thai basil leaves

Pork was quite pricey in Thailand, so to make a dish that would fill us all up, my mum would buy rice vermicelli, which she would soak in water in order to expand it. She then whipped up a simple stir-fry sauce, added the minuscule amount of pork and voilà – a hearty meal that would feed the whole family. Thrifty perfection!

Soak the rice vermicelli in a large bowl of warm water for about 5 minutes to soften.

Heat the oil in a wok set over a high heat. When hot, add the garlic and stir-fry for 5–10 seconds until fragrant. Add the pork, reduce the heat to medium and stir-fry for about 2–3 minutes until the meat is cooked.

Add the soy sauce, fish sauce, sugar and white pepper. Cook for a minute, then stir in the drained vermicelli and stir-fry for a further couple of minutes. Serve garnished with basil leaves.

SWEET
THINGS

BANANA BALLS

MAKES ABOUT 10

475ml (16fl oz) vegetable
   oil, for deep-frying
4 small bananas, cut into
   3.5cm (1½ inch) chunks
2 tablespoons honey, to serve

FOR THE BATTER

2 tablespoons sugar
200g (7oz) glutinous rice flour
200g (7oz) cornflour
½ teaspoon salt
1 teaspoon baking powder
1 egg, beaten
2 tablespoons evaporated milk
2 tablespoons melted butter

When I was little girl this was our staple dessert, which
we bought incredibly cheaply at the market. I learned
how to make it in school when I was about 14, so when
I eat this, it takes me back to the classroom.

First make the batter. Sift the dry ingredients into a mixing bowl,
then pour in the egg, evaporated milk and melted butter. Stir
only until the dry ingredients are moistened.

Heat the oil in a pan or stable wok over a medium heat. When
hot, dip the banana chunks, one by one, into the batter, ensuring
they are evenly covered, then immerse into the hot oil. Deep-
fry for 3 minutes, turning frequently, until golden brown all
over. Drain on kitchen paper, then serve drizzled with honey.

MANGO AND STICKY RICE

SERVES 2

200g (7oz) Thai sticky rice

100g (3½oz) granulated sugar

1 teaspoon salt

325ml (11fl oz) coconut milk

2 ripe yellow mangoes

2 sprigs of sweet basil,
   to decorate

Also known as sweet rice or glutinous rice, Thai sticky rice makes for a delicious dessert. Use black sticky rice (or a mixture of black and white) if you like a bit of visual drama. For best results, cook the rice in a steamer or a double-boiler.

Place the rice in a bowl, cover with cold water and leave to soak for 2–3 hours. Using a sieve, strain the soaked rice, then place it in a steamer or the top half of a double-boiler. Cover and steam over a high heat for 25–30 minutes, until soft and translucent.

Pour 250ml (8½fl oz) of the coconut milk into a small mixing bowl. Add the sugar and salt, stirring until they dissolve. Add the cooked sticky rice and stir until well mixed. Cover and leave to stand for 15 minutes.

Meanwhile, peel and slice the mangoes and set aside.

Place the remaining coconut milk in a small saucepan, bring to the boil, then take off the heat.

Divide the rice between 2 serving plates and top with the mango slices. Spoon over 3 tablespoons of the hot coconut milk and finish off with a sprig of basil.

COCONUT CUSTARD

SERVES 4

I small pumpkin

2 eggs, beaten

3 tablespoons palm sugar

3 tablespoons white sugar

200ml (7fl oz) thick
   coconut cream

This particular dish goes back to my childhood. Wonderfully thick and sweet, coconut custard is to Thailand what vanilla custard is to Britain. This dessert is best served cold, with the custard completely set and the pumpkin cut into wedges.

Slice off the top off the pumpkin and scoop out the seeds, leaving the flesh intact. Set aside.

Combine the eggs and sugars in a bowl. Stir until the sugar dissolves. Add the coconut cream and stir well. Pour the mixture into the hollowed pumpkin.

Prepare a steamer. When the water boils, place the pumpkin in the top half, then cover and steam for 45 minutes until the custard is set – test it carefully with a skewer. Leave to cool completely before serving.

TARO BALLS IN COCONUT SYRUP

SERVES 2

300g (10oz) taro root, scrubbed, rinsed, peeled and cut into chunks

4 tablespoons rice flour

200ml (7fl oz) coconut milk, plus 3 extra tablespoons

3 tablespoons cornflour

100ml (3½fl oz) water

5 tablespoons sugar

Pinch of salt

Dried coconut flakes, to garnish

I'm going to be honest here: taro balls are time-consuming to prepare. Whenever my parents had certain friends over, they would ask for this dish for dessert, and I would then spend hours rolling taro balls, which was probably the most mundane culinary experience ever – I'd rather peel potatoes! The effort is worth it, though, as this dish is delicious.

Prepare a steamer. When the water boils, place the taro root in the top half, cover and steam for about 5 minutes until the taro is tender. Transfer to a bowl, leave to cool a little, then mash it with a fork. Add the rice flour and the 3 tablespoons coconut milk, knead the mixture to form a dough.

Pinch off small pieces of the mixture and roll between your palms into 1cm (½ inch) balls. Put the cornflour on plate and roll the balls in it (this will prevent them from sticking together or to your hands). Set the prepared balls aside.

Combine the 200ml (7fl oz) coconut milk, measurement water, sugar and salt in a saucepan over a medium heat, stirring occasionally until the sugar has dissolved.

Increase the heat and bring the coconut milk mixture to the boiling point. Add the prepared taro balls and boil for 10–15 minutes until well cooked – they should be firm but chewy. Remove from the heat, spoon the taro balls into a bowl with some of the cooking syrup and serve hot or cold, sprinkled with coconut flakes.

FRESH FRUIT WITH COCONUT SYRUP

SERVES 4

5–6 tablespoons
   granulated sugar

400ml (14fl oz) coconut milk

Pinch of salt

½ small honeydew melon,
   peeled, deseeded and
   cut into chunks

½ cantaloupe melon,
   peeled, deseeded and
   cut into chunks

½ ripe papaya, peeled,
   deseeded and cut
   into chunks

2 slices of fresh pineapple,
   cut into chunks

Large handful of crushed ice

There was a never-ending supply of melons at my family's farm in Thailand: they grew all around the edges of the property. As a result, we would take turns trying to come up with new ways of using them – this recipe is one of those ideas.

Put the sugar and coconut milk in a small saucepan set over a medium heat, stirring until the sugar has dissolved. Add a pinch of salt and boil for 5 minutes or until the mixture forms a syrup. Set aside to cool completely.

Arrange the melon, papaya and pineapple pieces in serving bowls. Pour over the syrup, then top with crushed ice. Serve immediately.

COCONUT PUDDING

MAKES ABOUT 20

6–8 long, broad pandan
  leaves (available from Asian
  supermarkets), to serve

Pineapple pieces, to decorate

FOR THE BOTTOM LAYER

3 tablespoons rice flour

2 tablespoons cornflour

3½ tablespoons
  granulated sugar

250ml (8fl oz) water

50g (2oz) canned water
  chestnuts, drained
  and chopped

FOR THE TOP LAYER

2 tablespoon rice flour

2 tablespoons cornflour

200ml (7fl oz) coconut milk

1 teaspoon salt

My auntie had a dessert stall in our village market and I used to help her out sometimes when I was young. This dish was my wages. I didn't care about being paid, because I would have used the money to buy coconut pudding anyway – that's how much I loved it. The little pandan leaf cups are easier to make than you might think, and so pretty that they're well worth the trouble, but you can serve this dessert in very small cups or bowls instead.

To make pandan leaf serving cups, trim the ends off the leaves then cut each one into pieces 16cm (6½ inches) long. Take a piece of leaf and make 4 evenly spaced cuts into the long side, cutting about halfway into the leaf – these four 'tabs' will form the floor of the cup. Now bring the short ends of the leaf together, folding up the four 'tabs' as you do so to make the base. Secure at the side with a staple.

To make the bottom layer of the pudding, combine the rice flour, cornflour, sugar and water in a saucepan and place over a medium-high heat. Add the water chestnuts and stir until the sugar has dissolved. Reduce the heat to low and continue stirring for about 5 minutes until the sauce has thickened (it should have the consistency of thick custard). Take the pan off the heat and set aside.

Now make the top layer. Combine the rice flour, cornflour, coconut milk and salt in a saucepan. Place over a medium-low heat and stir continuously for about 5–7 minutes until the mixture has thickened. f you wish, you can add a few slivers of leftover pandan leaf to the mixture for extra flavour and fragrance.

Carefully place a spoonful of chestnut mixture in each leaf cup, then spoon the coconut milk mixture over the top. Set aside to cool completely. Serve topped with a piece of pineapple. These puddings will keep in the refrigerator for 2 days.

BANANA FRITTERS WITH COCONUT BATTER

SERVES 2–4

300g (10oz) rice flour

400ml (14fl oz) tablespoons coconut milk

50g (2oz) granulated sugar

125g (4oz) fresh shredded coconut

1 teaspoon nigella seeds

6 small bananas

475ml (16fl oz) vegetable oil, for deep-frying

Honey or ice cream, to serve

The bananas in Thailand are much smaller and a lot sweeter than the ones you get in Europe. They are also grown in such large quantities that banana fritters are probably the most widely eaten dessert in the country. It's so fresh and simple – you just dip a banana in batter and deep-fry it - but I can't say it's exactly healthy. This is a treat for special occasions.

Put the flour and coconut milk into a bowl and mix well to form a smooth batter. Stir in the sugar, then the coconut and the nigella seeds. Add a little water if the batter is too thick – you want it to be nice and gloopy.

Peel the bananas and cut them in half lengthways. Now put the oil in a wok over a medium heat. When the oil is hot, coat the banana in the batter, then gently place a few at a time in the oil. Deep-fry for about 10 minutes until golden brown all over. Remove the fritters and drain on kitchen paper. Serve drizzled with honey or with a bowl of ice cream.

BASICS

RED
CURRY PASTE
202

YELLOW
CURRY PASTE
202

GREEN
CURRY PASTE
203

MASSAMAN
CURRY PASTE
203

JUNGLE
CURRY PASTE
204

PENANG
CURRY PASTE
204

BEEF BASE FOR
NOODLE SOUP
207

THAI CHICKEN STOCK
207

TAMARIND SAUCE
208

MY MOTHER'S
SIRICHA
208

SWEET
CHILLI SAUCE
210

ROASTED
CHILLI SAUCE
210

FRESH SPRING ROLL
SAUCE
211

THAI MARINADE SAUCE
211

THAI SEAFOOD DRESSING
212

BEEF SALAD DRESSING
212

SAIPHIN SAUCE
213

GINGER TEA
216

LEMON GRASS TEA
217

RED CURRY PASTE

I come from a Lao family, but whenever we wanted to cook Thai food, we never bought ready-made paste. Instead, we made our own from scratch, using ingredients from our herb garden at the back of the house. I used to hate making curry paste as we had only a wooden mortar and pestle, so it would take what seemed like forever to grind down. A food processor makes things much faster!

MAKES 125ML (4FL OZ)

5 dried red spur chillies, deseeded
   and soaked until tender
I teaspoon sea salt
I teaspoon galangal, finely sliced
2 tablespoons lesser galangal
2 lemon grass stalks, sliced
I teaspoon finely grated makrut lime zest
2 teaspoons sliced coriander root
10 small garlic cloves
$^1/_3$ shallot, sliced
I tablespoon coriander seeds, roasted and ground
I teaspoon cumin seeds, roasted and ground
I teaspoon shrimp paste

Finely grind the chillies and salt together using a mortar and pestle or a food processor. When you have a fine paste, add the galangals, lemon grass, lime zest and coriander root. Blend again or pound to a fine paste.

Dry fry the coriander and cumin seeds for 2 minutes, until fragrant, stirring continuously. Pound or grind to a powder.

Add the garlic, shallot, ground seeds and shrimp paste. Continue to blend or pound until smooth.

This curry paste will keep in the refrigerator for 4–8 weeks if stored in an airtight container, and for up to 6 months in the freezer.

YELLOW CURRY PASTE

I ate Yellow Curry for the first time when I visited a friend in Hong Kong. She made the paste herself, inspiring me with her creativity.

MAKES APPROXIMATELY 250ML (8FL OZ)

5 shallots, unpeeled
10 small garlic cloves, unpeeled
2 tablespoons finely sliced galangal
I teaspoon finely sliced fresh root ginger
I tablespoon coriander seeds
3 dried red spur chillies, deseeded
   and soaked until tender
I teaspoon sea salt
2 tablespoons sliced lemon grass
I teaspoon ground cumin
2 teaspoons curry powder
I teaspoon shrimp paste

In a wok or frying pan, dry-fry the whole shallots and garlic, until golden and soft. This will take 5–10 minutes. Set aside to cool, then peel off the skin.

Dry-fry the galangal and ginger for 2-3 minutes over a medium heat until fragrant and slightly golden. Remove from the pan and set aside.

Dry-fry the coriander seeds for about 2 minutes, stirring continuously, until fragrant. Grind or pound until fine.

Finely pound or blend the chillies and salt. Add the roasted galangal and ginger plus the lemon grass and blend or pound well. Add the shallots and garlic and blend or pound again. Add the ground coriander seeds, cumin, curry powder and shrimp paste and mix until smooth.

GREEN CURRY PASTE

My Thai auntie was a huge inspiration in terms of the food we cooked at home in Laos. She came from Phitsanulok in central Thailand, and brought many recipes and ingredients into our home. She taught me so much, and I loved to cook with her. Once a month we would go to the temple, and she always cooked a delicious green curry, using homemade curry paste.

....

MAKES 150ML (¼ PINT)

1 teaspoon sea salt
5 long green chillies, sliced
5 green spur chillies, sliced
3 tablespoons galangal, finely sliced
2 tablespoons sliced lesser galangal
3 lemon grass stalks, sliced
1 tablespoon finely grated lime zest
3 coriander roots, finely sliced
4 shallots, sliced
1 garlic clove
1 teaspoon shrimp paste
1 tablespoon coriander seeds, roasted and ground
1 teaspoon cumin seeds, roasted and ground
5 black peppercorns, crushed

Finely grind the salt and chillies together using a mortar and pestle or a food processor. When you have a smooth paste, add the galangals, lemon grass, lime zest and coriander roots. Grind or blend well, then add the shallots, garlic, shrimp paste, ground seeds and peppercorns. Blend or grind to a smooth paste.

This curry paste will keep in the refrigerator for 4–8 weeks if stored in an airtight container, and for up to 6 months in the freezer.

MASSAMAN CURRY PASTE

To make this curry paste, you will need to dry-fry or roast many of the ingredients before pounding them into a paste – this gives Massaman curry its distinctive taste.

....

MAKES 150ML (¼ PINT)

5 shallots, unpeeled
2 heads of garlic, unpeeled
2 tablespoons sliced galangal
1 lemon grass stalk, sliced
1 tablespoon coriander seeds
1 teaspoon cumin seeds
2 cloves
1 teaspoon peppercorns
3 dried red spur chillies, deseeded and soaked until tender
1 teaspoon sea salt
1 teaspoon ground cardamom
1 teaspoon shrimp paste

In a wok or frying pan, dry-fry the whole shallots and garlic for 5–10 minutes until golden and soft. Set aside to cool, then peel off the skin.

Dry-fry the galangal and lemon grass over a medium heat until fragrant and slightly golden, about 2–3 minutes. Set aside. Dry-fry the coriander seeds, cumin, cloves and peppercorns for 2 minutes, until fragrant, stirring continuously. Pound or grind to a powder.

Finely pound or grind the chillies and salt. Add the roasted galangal and lemon grass and pound or grind well. Add the shallots and garlic and continue to pound or grind, then add the ground roasted spices, the cardamom and the shrimp paste. Mix until smooth.

JUNGLE CURRY PASTE

When I was a little girl, I used to have dinner at the house of one of my best friends. The family would make a curry that didn't have coconut milk in it, so the paste had to be slightly different than usual, and they would always ask me to make the curry paste. My friend's mother told me that the quicker and louder you bashed the ingredients in the mortar, the more the boys would fall in love with you. At the time I believed her, but now I realize it was just because she wanted me to hurry up so she could eat!

MAKES APPROXIMATELY 250ML (8FL OZ)

5 dried red spur chillies, deseeded and
    soaked until tender
20 dried hot chillies
20 small fresh hot chillies of assorted colours
I teaspoon sea salt
3 lemon grass stalks, sliced
2 teaspoons finely grated makrut lime zest
2 tablespoons galangal, finely chopped
I head of garlic, cloves separated
5 shallots, sliced
I tablespoon shrimp paste
I teaspoon black peppercorns

Finely pound or grind all the chillies with the salt. Once smooth, add the lemon grass, lime zest and galangal and pound again. Add the garlic, shallots, shrimp paste and black peppercorns and continue to pound or grind until you have a smooth paste.

This curry paste will keep in the refrigerator for 4–8 weeks if stored in an airtight container, and for up to 6 months in the freezer.

PENANG CURRY PASTE

This is another recipe that my Thai auntie passed down to me and it was used to make my favourite curry when I was a little girl. There was a local market stall that was open from 5 a.m. every day. I loved the stall and the Penang curry it served so much that the owner even allowed me to help out there when I was a young girl. I still love this curry today.

MAKES APPROXIMATELY 100ML (3½FL OZ)

5 dried red spur chillies, deseeded
    and soaked until tender
I teaspoon sea salt
2 tablespoons finely sliced galangal
2 tablespoons lesser galangal
3 lemon grass stalks, sliced
½ tablespoon finely sliced makrut lime zest
I tablespoon finely sliced coriander root
4 shallots, chopped
10 small garlic cloves, chopped
½ teaspoon black peppercorns
I teaspoon shrimp paste

Finely grind or pound the chillies and salt until you have a fine paste. Add the galangals, lemon grass, lime zest and coriander root. Grind or pound until you have a smooth paste, then add the shallots, garlic, peppercorns and shrimp paste. Grind or pound again until smooth.

This curry paste will keep in the refrigerator for 4–8 weeks if stored in an airtight container, and for up to 6 months in the freezer.

BEEF BASE FOR NOODLE SOUP

I'm a huge fan of noodle soup. Even now, I eat noodles every morning, just as many would eat cereal for breakfast. This base can be used for any kind of noodle soup – try a variation of the Chicken Noodle Soup on page 66.

....

SERVES 4–5

500ml (17fl oz) water
300g (10oz) oxtail
2 lemon grass stalks, chopped
5 thin slices of galangal
2 long pandan leaves (available
    from Asian supermarkets)
200g (7oz) pineapple, cubed
1 tablespoon oyster sauce
1 tablespoon palm sugar
3 tablespoons light soy sauce
1 teaspoon dark soy sauce
3 star anise
1 cinnamon stick
1 teaspoon salt
1 teaspoon black peppercorns

Pour the water into a deep saucepan, then add everything else – just chuck it all in. Set the pan over a high heat and bring to a rolling boil, then cover and simmer for 45 minutes. There's no need to stir; just leave the soup to simmer until it becomes clear.

The noodle soup base will keep in the fridge for 3–4 days, or can be frozen in individual portions for 2–3 months.

THAI CHICKEN STOCK

There is always a pan of chicken stock on my stove. This recipe comes from my home town and has been with me for as long as I can remember, but feel free to tweak it as you wish. Bear in mind that it should have a neutral taste so that it doesn't overpower the dish you add it to.

....

MAKES 5.2 LITRES (9 PINTS)

5 litres (8¾ pints) water
1 chicken carcass
1 tablespoon palm sugar
2½ teaspoons salt
5 coriander roots
3 whole pickled garlic cloves
1 daikon, halved
1 pandan leaf
1 teaspoon ground pepper
4 tablespoons light soy sauce

Bring the water to the boil in a large pan and add the chicken carcass along with the remaining ingredients in the order listed above.

Bring to a slow boil and boil for 10 minutes. Reduce the heat and simmer covered for 40 minutes. Strain, discarding the solids.

The stock can be stored in the fridge for 3–4 days, or in the freezer for 2–3 months.

TAMARIND SAUCE

Tamarind is a very popular fruit in Thailand. Phetchabun, my province, is well known for its tamarind produce, and people travel from far and wide to obtain this extremely tangy fruit. It can be used to give dishes – most notably, Pad Thai – fantastic flavour.

....

MAKES 300ML (½ PINT)

100g (3½oz) tamarind pulp
250ml (8fl oz) warm water
4 tablespoons demerara sugar
1 teaspoon chilli powder
50ml (2fl oz) light soy sauce
1 teaspoon dark soy sauce
2 tablespoons fried onion (available
    ready-to-use from Asian supermarkets,
    or you can prepare your own)

Soak the tamarind pulp in a saucepan in the warm water for around 2 minutes, then stir until it becomes a thick liquid. Set the pan over a medium heat.

Add the sugar, chilli powder and soy sauces, then heat, stirring continuously, until the mixture thickens, about 2–3 minutes.

Finally, add the onion, stir for around 10 minutes, then take the pan off the heat and leave to stand for 5 minutes. The sauce should taste sweet and sour, with a tangy aftertaste.

Store in an airtight container in the refrigerator and use within 4 weeks.

MY MOTHER'S SIRICHA

You may have heard of a spicy red sauce labelled 'siricha' or 'sriracha', but – however it's spelt – the name encompasses a range of different sauces. My mum gave me this recipe, so I have never had to buy the sauce. In my opinion, this version is the best!

....

MAKES 500ML (17FL OZ)

5 long red Thai chillies, roughly chopped
1 red romano pepper, roughly chopped
10 garlic cloves
250ml (8fl oz) white vinegar
2 tablespoons granulated sugar
2 tablespoons salt

Put all the ingredients in a blender and process to make a sauce. Pour the mixture into a small saucepan and cook over a medium heat for 5 minutes until it has thickened. Serve at room temperature.

Store the sauce in an airtight container in the refrigerator and use within 4 weeks.

SWEET CHILLI SAUCE

In Thailand this sauce is used with everything, everywhere! It is especially popular in my home town, where it's renowned for being extra spicy.

....

MAKES 400–500ML (14–17FL OZ)

150g (5oz) cubed pineapple

10 long red chillies

2 red peppers

10 garlic cloves

2 lemon grass stalks, chopped

1 tablespoon crushed galangal

150ml (¼ pint) rice vinegar

1 teaspoon salt

3 tablespoons palm sugar

3 tablespoons demerara sugar

1 tablespoon cornflour

Blend the pineapple, chillies, peppers, garlic, lemon grass and galangal in a blender or using a pestle and mortar until a very fine paste. Set aside.

Set a deep saucepan over a high heat and add the rice vinegar, followed by the salt and sugars. Stir constantly until everything has dissolved, then slowly mix in the pineapple paste one tablespoon at a time. Cook over a gentle heat, adding the cornflour a teaspoon at a time until the sauce has your desired thickness.

Store the sauce in an airtight container in the refrigerator and use within 4 weeks.

ROASTED CHILLI SAUCE

I moved to Hong Kong when I was still a teenager and, being 19, I would go out for a couple of drinks with my friends in the evening. Quite often, the night would end with us turning up at the same noodle shop at 4 a.m. to consume some of the most fantastic noodles ever made, accompanied by a great fiery sauce. This is my take on that sauce. The noodle shop has no name, but I'm sure that if you ever go out in Hong Kong with a local, you might very well end up there.

....

MAKES 300ML (½ PINT)

5 tablespoons chilli flakes

1 tablespoon chopped garlic

2 teaspoons chopped red onion

2 teaspoons pounded dried shrimp

3 teaspoons vegetable oil

1 teaspoon sugar

1 teaspoon nam pla (Thai fish sauce)

Dry-fry the chilli flakex, garlic and onion in a frying pan for 3–5 minutes or until cooked. Add the dried shrimp, mix to a paste and take the pan off the heat.

In a separate frying pan, heat the oil over a medium-high heat, then fry the paste you have just made until it is brown. Add the sugar and fish sauce.

Store the sauce in an airtight container in the refrigerator and use within 4 weeks.

FRESH SPRING ROLL SAUCE

When I lived in Hong Kong, a friend once asked me to help her prepare fresh spring rolls for a party. She made a sauce for them that was delicious, so I asked her for the recipe. A few years later, when I was back in my home town in Thailand, I decided to tweak the recipe, and the sweet yet tangy taste of tamarind, a speciality product of my province, gave it the perfect twist.

MAKES 600ML (I PINT)

400g (I3oz) tamarind pulp

I litre (I¾ pints) water

I0 tablespoons sugar

5 tablespoons palm sugar

5 tablespoons light soy sauce

5 tablespoons sweet soy sauce (available from Chinese supermarkets)

3 tablespoons finely chopped pickled garlic

I teaspoon chilli powder

I tablespoon salt

50 g (2 oz) roasted peanuts, crushed

Soak the tamarind pulp in a deep saucepan in the warm water for around 2 minutes, then stir until it becomes a thick liquid.

Set the pan over a medium heat. Add the sugars and heat gently, stirring continuously until the sugars have dissolved. Stir in the soy sauces, garlic, chilli powder and salt as you go along. The sauce should be thick, gloopy and syrupy.

Finally, add the peanuts and stir well.

Store the sauce in an airtight container in the refrigerator and use within 4 weeks.

THAI MARINADE SAUCE

In my village we never grilled any meat without marinating it first, and this is the marinade recipe that has stuck with me since I was a child. It is so simple to make, yet so delicious, bringing depth of flavour to a dish and tenderizing meat wonderfully.

MAKES I50ML (¼ PINT)

50g (2oz) fresh pineapple, blended to a pulp

I tablespoon light soy sauce

I teaspoon granulated sugar

I teaspoon white pepper powder

Mix the all ingredients together in a bowl until the sugar has dissolved.

Marinate any kind of meat in this sauce for I5–20 minutes. The acid in the pineapple pulp will tenderize it and impart a melt-in-the-mouth texture.

THAI SEAFOOD DRESSING

The beauty of this sauce is that no matter where or who you are in Thailand, your family will have their unique take on the recipe. It's the type of a dish you show off to other families. This is my family's version – a perfect dipping sauce for steamed fish, grilled chicken or barbecued pork – pretty much everything. The most important thing to remember is that it works best with my Spicy Seafood Salad (see page 42).

....

MAKES 300ML (½ PINT)

3 tablespoons nam pla (Thai fish sauce)

3 tablespoons lime juice

1½ tablespoons sugar

2 tablespoons evaporated milk

Combine the fish sauce, lime juice and sugar in a small dish. Stir until the sugar dissolves, then mix in the evaporated milk. The dressing will keep in the fridge for up to week, stored in an airtight jar, but it's best made fresh when you need it.

BEEF SALAD DRESSING

Whenever we had a big family party, perhaps if someone was getting married or one of the men was becoming a monk, I used to make beef salad and this dressing, All the women would help prepare the vegetables, chatting away about the event being celebrated. I would always be in there, squeezing the lime juice or peeling the garlic. This sauce therefore always reminds me of everyone being together in the party spirit. Depending on how much time you have, you can use ready-made siricha sauce and sweet chilli sauce for this recipe, or you can make your own (see pages 208 and 210).

....

MAKES 150ML (¼ PINT)

3 tablespoon nam pla (Thai fish sauce)

3 tablespoons lime juice

2 tablespoons siricha sauce

1½ tablespoons sugar

2 tablespoons sweet chilli sauce

Combine the fish sauce, lime juice, siricha and sugar in a small dish. Stir until the sugar dissolves, then add the sweet chilli sauce.

SAIPHIN SAUCE

I adore balsamic vinegar. In Thailand we usually use rice vinegar, so when I first tried balsamic vinegar in Hong Kong I loved it and immediately bought myself a bottle. This sauce is a perfect dressing for all kinds of salads, from tomato to beef. You can make a large quantity and store it in the fridge in an airtight container, but it is best made fresh.

....

MAKES 250ML (8FL OZ)

5 red spur chillies, sliced

4 garlic cloves, crushed

2 coriander roots, crushed (if you can't find roots, use coriander stalks)

1 teaspoon salt

1 teaspoon granulated sugar

3 tablespoons lime juice

3 tablespoons olive oil

3 tablespoons balsamic vinegar

Pound or process the chillies, garlic and coriander roots into a paste, then add the remaining ingredients and stir well.

GINGER TEA

SERVES 2

1 litre (1¾ pints) water

65g (2½oz) fresh root ginger, peeled and thinly sliced

1 tablespoon brown sugar

Sugar syrup (see opposite) or extra sugar (optional)

My home town is located high in the hilltops in a vast mountainous area that has scattered populations of Hmong people. They would grow ginger and we would buy it from them and sell it on to the people down below. If we had any left over, we would make this simple drink. It is best served on a cold winter's day, but ginger tea is also good served chilled.

Bring the measurement water to the boil in a saucepan. Add the ginger and boil for 15 minutes, no longer or the flavour of the ginger will be weakened.

Stir in the sugar and serve. If you like your ginger tea a little sweeter, add some sugar syrup or more sugar.

LEMON GRASS TEA

SERVES 4-5

2 lemon grass stalks, chopped
   into 6cm (2 ½ inch) pieces
I litre (I¾ pints) water

FOR THE SUGAR SYRUP
250ml (8fl oz) water
5 tablespoons granulated sugar

Lemon grass is extremely popular in Thailand and is considered to have medicinal properties. It is used to heal all sorts of ailments, but I use it mainly to feel happy. It has a wonderful aroma and unique flavour, and is packed full of antioxidants. I highly recommended it after a filling meal.

First make the syrup: heat the measurement water in a small saucepan over a medium heat, add the sugar and stir to dissolve. Remove from the heat and set aside.

To make the tea, smash the lemon grass using a pestle and mortar.

Bring the water to the boil in a saucepan. Add the lemon grass and boil for 10 minutes. Serve immediately with the sugar syrup on the side, and sweeten to taste.

INDEX

ACKNOWLEDGEMENTS

I'd like to say thank you to everyone who has ever supported me. To my family, I owe the world: my grandparents, my mum and dad, my sisters Tabtim and Kratin and my brother Padon, my uncle Cambrung and my auntie – every single person in my family who has given me support, be it moral or through actually teaching me the many recipes in this book all those years ago. These recipes do not all come from the top of my head, of course, and without these unsung master chefs I truly believe I wouldn't be where I am today. I am forever grateful.

Thank you also to my wonderful children – Newton, Natalie, Noah and Richard. Another thank you goes to the incredibly supportive Rosa's team and Kate Towers, and of course to my darling husband, Alex Moore, without whom none of this would ever have happened. I would also like to say a big thank you to Gaby and Jonathan Alexander, who have been so supportive since I moved to London, and to John Conyngham, who was there for me from the very start of Rosa's. And of course thank you to the Octopus team, who have done so much to help me with this book. I couldn't have done it without you.

Last but not least, I want to say an extra-big thank you to my co-writer and son, Richard Poole, who has helped me from day one till the book was done – he is my clone.

Thank you, everyone!

Saiphin

Visit us at www.rosasthaicafe.com

Follow us on Twitter @RosasThaiCafe

Email us at SayHelloToSaiphin@rosaslondon.com